REDFIELD LIBRARY
DATE DUE

081410			
GAYLORD			PRINTED IN U.S.A.

PIONEERS in SCIENCE

SPACE AND ASTRONOMY

The People Behind the Science

SCOTT MCCUTCHEON AND BOBBI MCCUTCHEON

CHELSEA HOUSE
PUBLISHERS
An imprint of Infobase Publishing

*We dedicate this book to
all future pioneers in science.*

Space and Astronomy: The People Behind the Science

Copyright © 2006 by Scott McCutcheon and Bobbi McCutcheon

Chelsea House
An imprint of Infobase Publishing
132 West 31st Street
New York NY 10001

Library of Congress Cataloging-in-Publication Data

McCutcheon, Scott.
    Space and astronomy: the people behind the science / Scott McCutcheon and Bobbi McCutcheon
        p. cm. — (Pioneers in science)
    ISBN 0-8160-5467-3 (hardcover)
    1. Astronomy—History—Juvenile literature. 2. Astronomers—Biography—Juvenile literature. I. McCutcheon, Bobbi. II. Title III. Series.
    QB46.M17 2005
    520'.92'2—dc22   2004023513

Chelsea House books are available at special discounts when purchased in bulk quantities for businesses, associations, institutions, or sales promotions. Please call our Special Sales Department in New York at (212) 967-8800 or (800) 322-8755.

You can find Chelsea House on the World Wide Web at
http://www.chelseahouse.com

Text design by Mary Susan Ryan-Flynn
Cover design by Cathy Rincon
Illustrations by Bobbi McCutcheon

Printed in the United States of America

MP FOF 10 9 8 7 6 5 4 3 2 1

This book is printed on acid-free paper.

CONTENTS

CHAPTER 3

Galileo Galilei (1564–1642): Physicist Revolutionizes Astronomical Observation with the Newly Invented Telescope   34

CHAPTER 4

Johannes Kepler (1571–1630): The Father of Celestial Mechanics   51

CHAPTER 5
Benjamin Banneker (1731–1806): The First African-American Astronomer   69

CHAPTER 6
Sir William Herschel (1738–1822): The Father of Sidereal Astronomy   84

CHAPTER 7

Robert H. Goddard (1882–1945): The Father of Modern Rocketry and Space Flight

CHAPTER 8

Wernher von Braun (1912–1977): The Twentieth Century's Foremost Rocket Engineer

CHAPTER 9

Carl Sagan (1934–1996): Modern Popularizer of Space Science and Cofounder of the New Field of Exobiology   138

CHAPTER 10

Stephen Hawking (1942–): The Modern Einstein   156

PREFACE

Being first in line earns a devoted fan the best seat in the stadium. The first runner to break the ribbon spanning the finish line receives a gold medal. The firstborn child inherits the royal throne. Certain advantages or privileges often accompany being the first, but sometimes the price paid is considerable. Neil Armstrong, the first man to walk on the Moon, began flying lessons at age 16, toiled at numerous jobs to pay tuition, studied diligently to earn his bachelor's degree in aerospace engineering, flew 78 combat missions in Korea as a brave navy pilot, worked as a civilian test pilot for seven years, then as an astronaut for NASA for another seven years, and made several dangerous trips into space before the historic *Apollo 11* mission. He endured rigorous physical and mental preparation, underwent years of training, and risked his life to courageously step foot where no man had ever walked before. Armstrong was a pioneer of space exploration; he opened up the way for others to follow. Not all pioneering activities may be as perilous as space exploration. But like the ardent fan, a pioneer in science must be dedicated; like the competitive runner, he or she must be committed; and like being born to royalty, sometimes providence plays a role.

Science encompasses all knowledge based on general truths or observed facts. More narrowly defined, science refers to a branch of knowledge that specifically deals with the natural world and its laws. Philosophically described, science is an endeavor, a search for truth, a way of knowing, or a means of discovering. Scientists gain information through employing a procedure called the scientific method. The scientific method requires one to state the problem and formulate a testable hypothesis or educated guess to describe a phenomenon or explain an observation, test the hypothesis experimentally or by collecting data from observations, and draw conclusions from the results. Data can eliminate a hypothesis, but never confirm it with absolute certainty; scientists may accept a hypothesis as true when sufficient supporting evidence has been obtained. The process sounds entirely straightforward, but sometimes advancements in science do not follow such a logical approach. Because humans make the observations, generate the hypothesis, carry out the experiments, and draw the conclusions, students of science must recognize the personal dimension of science.

Pioneers in Science is a set of volumes that profiles the people behind the science, individuals who initiated new lines of thought or research. They risked possible failure and often faced opposition but persisted to pave new pathways of scientific exploration. Their backgrounds vary tremendously; some never graduated from secondary school, while others earned multiple advanced degrees. Familial affluence allowed some to pursue research unhindered by financial concerns, but others were so poor they suffered from malnutrition or became homeless. Personalities ranged from exuberant to somber and gentle to stubborn, but they all sacrificed, giving their time, insight, and commitment because they believed in the pursuit of knowledge. The desire to understand kept them going when they faced difficulties, and their contributions moved science forward.

The set consists of eight separate volumes: *Biology; Chemistry; Earth Science; Marine Science; Physics; Science, Technology, and Society; Space and Astronomy;* and *Weather and Climate.* Each book contains 10 biographical sketches of pioneering individuals in a subject, including information about their childhood, how they entered into their scientific careers, their research, and enough background science information for the reader to appreciate their discoveries and contributions. Though all the profiled individuals are certainly distinguished, their inclusion is not intended to imply that they are the greatest scientists of all time. Rather, the profiled individuals were selected to reflect a variety of subdisciplines in each field, different histories, alternative approaches to science, and diverse characters. Each chapter includes a chronology and a list of specific references about the individual and his or her work. Each book also includes an introduction to the field of science to which its pioneers contributed, line illustrations, photographs, a glossary of scientific terms related to the research described in the text, and a listing of further resources for information about the general subject matter.

The goal of this set is to provide, at an appropriate level, factual information about pioneering scientists. The authors hope that readers will be inspired to achieve greatness themselves, to feel connected to the people behind science, and to believe that they may have a positive and enduring impact on society.

ACKNOWLEDGMENTS

As the authors of this volume, we would like to express our deepest appreciation to executive editor Frank K. Darmstadt for his invaluable guidance, to copy editor Laura Magzis, and to the production department for its generous help in editing the text and illustrations, respectively, for the entire Pioneers in Science set. To our associate, author Dr. Katherine Cullen, we convey our most heartfelt admiration and sincerest gratitude for her assistance in putting our book together. We would like to extend a very special thanks to world-renowned author and historian Silvio A. Bedini for taking the time to speak with us about 18th-century astronomy. To the Cornell University Library, we offer appreciation for answering our questions and conducting research on our behalf. Special indebtedness goes out to the librarians at the University of Alaska Southeast and the Juneau Public Library for granting renewals, placing interlibrary loans, and their general fine handling of the many reference materials we used during our research process. We would like to recognize all agencies for providing the photographs, some free of charge, that appear in this book and a personal thank-you to photographer Larry Adkins for going the extra mile to provide necessary images. In conclusion, we warmly acknowledge all the authors and organizations mentioned throughout the book and in the Further Resources section, without whom this book could not be possible.

INTRODUCTION

Astronomy is, perhaps arguably, the oldest science. For thousands of years and all across the globe, humankind has observed the stars as they wheel overhead in the night sky. Some studied the stars merely out of the love of their beauty. Others applied science to their observations by recording the path and positions of the planets and constellations as a way to keep track of the passage of time and to know when to expect the change in the seasons. In some civilizations, the reaping and sowing of crops depended entirely on the location of certain groups of stars. Early Egyptians, for example, based their calendar on the path of Sirius, the Dog Star. The day it first showed on the horizon, just prior to the rising of the Sun, marked the first day of the Egyptian New Year, since the appearance of Sirius always heralded the imminent flooding of the Nile.

In southern England, around 2900 B.C.E., as a way to keep track of the summer and winter solstices, the ancient Druids began to engineer the astronomical site we know today as Stonehenge. Some experts claim it took as much as 1,400 years of observations for these ancient people to arrange the stones exactly as they wanted them. Described by many as more than merely a temple to the Sun and Moon, Stonehenge is likely an ancient astronomical calculator capable of predicting astronomical events such as eclipses.

Indeed, the mysteriousness of an eclipse was of major concern for not just the Druids. Recorded astronomical observations found in the ancient Chinese civilizations are direct evidence of how these people carefully tracked and recorded each event in the hopes of predicting an eclipse before it ever happened. Chinese bone and shell inscriptions hold records of lunar and solar eclipses dating as far back as the 13th century B.C.E.

Beginning around 600 B.C.E., the influence of the Greeks became widespread across the lands of the Mediterranean, which was most of the known civilized world at that time. Their philosophies and mathematical skills were unsurpassed by any other culture. The Greek form of astronomy is well known today largely because their records endured, unlike other civilizations, such as the Maya or Inca, whose history is lost. The Greeks performed significant experiments and vastly superior observations. One result was the commonly accepted philosophy that the Earth was a stationary entity and all the heavens, including the Sun, revolved around it.

A different theory was proposed by some Greeks, such as Aristarchus, who stated that the Earth was not stationary but was itself in motion. This concept was not widely accepted due to the direct observation that, from the perspective of Earth, all other heavenly objects appeared in motion. Consequently, the idea that Earth was the center of the universe stood as absolute authority for 1,500 years until the 16th century C.E., when European astronomers began to revolutionize astronomical science through better observations and mathematical calculations.

From this point on, the history of astronomy has many turning points that resulted in different branches of the science other than the mere practice of tracking celestial movements in order to keep a calendar.

Today's modern astronomy encompasses such subfields as:

- Astrophysics: dealing with the physics of the universe
- Astrometry: dealing with the positions, motions, and distances of stars and planets
- Celestial mechanics: dealing with the application of Newtonian physics to the stars and planets
- Extragalactic astrophysics: dealing with the physics of galaxies outside our own
- Theoretical astrophysics: dealing with general relativity and cosmology

■ Planetary astronomy: dealing with theoretical modeling of planetary characteristics

This volume in the Pioneers in Science set profiles 10 scientists who contributed to the development of modern astronomy in different ways, beginning with the revolutionary heliocentric theory. The fact that the Sun was the center of the solar system was not fully accepted until the 17th century, roughly 100 years after Polish astronomer Nicolas Copernicus became the first to openly support a heliocentric theory of the solar system in his 1543 publication, *De revolutionibus orbium coelestium* (On the revolutions of the celestial orbits). Many innovative ideas took place during this European social transformation known as the Renaissance. In the mid-1500s, Danish astronomer Tycho Brahe built Europe's largest observatory and revolutionized techniques of celestial observation by developing fantastic precision instruments to measure the positions of the stars and planets in the night sky using only the naked eye (the development of the world's first observational telescope was still nearly four decades away).

After the invention of the telescope, knowledge of the universe began an even more radical change. Dutch scientist Hans Lippershey devised the first crude telescope in the early 17th century. Practically overnight, Galileo Galilei improved on Lippershey's design and changed the knowledge of the solar system by observing Jupiter's moons for the first time and by providing overwhelming proof in support of the Copernican theory. During this same era, German astronomer Johannes Kepler revolutionized the dynamics of the solar system by demonstrating that the planets moved in elliptical orbits, not in circular orbits, as was the standard belief up until his time. Kepler's discoveries, based on the intricate naked-eye observations set down by Tycho Brahe, led to the formulation of what are now known as Kepler's three laws of planetary motion. One hundred years later, during the 18th century, an African-American farmer named Benjamin Banneker taught himself astronomy and became the first African American to publish multiple sets of astronomical ephemerides that could predict eclipses and general weather conditions. Sir William Herschel was a German-born English astronomer of the late 1700s and early 1800s who applied a system to study the stars and their attributes, thus becoming the inventor of sidereal astronomy. He also developed superior telescopes and is the discoverer of the planet Uranus and the Orion Nebula.

The possible exploration of space beyond the use of ground-based telescopes became a reality in the early 1900s when American physicist Robert H. Goddard invented the first liquid-fueled rocket, capable of generating enough thrust to reach high altitudes. Within a few more years, German physicist Wernher von Braun organized the development of some of the first guided ballistic missiles, helped pioneer research into putting humans in orbit, and designed the largest superbooster ever built, the *Saturn V,* for the U.S. Apollo space program, which is responsible for putting the first men on the Moon.

In the 20th century, the idea of space travel became a reality, resulting in a new branch of space science. In the early 1950s, American astronomer Carl Sagan helped give rise to the field of exobiology, the scientific search for signs of life beyond Earth. He became famous for bringing his advocacy of exobiology to the public and for making it a serious science.

The search for life in space is not a small task due to the vastness of the universe, a vastness that is incomprehensible to most of us. There are cosmologists, such as British theoretical physicist Stephen Hawking, one of the world's top scientists of the modern era, who do understand it. Hawking has revolutionized cosmology by using applied mathematics to identify the existence and characteristics of black holes. Recently, he has conducted pioneering research into the quantum origin of the universe and has been working toward combining quantum mechanics and gravity into a unified theory of physics. He is also one of the major supporters of the modern big bang theory as the probable origin of the universe.

To a number of people, the immensity of the science of astronomy seems as intimidating as the voids of space itself. To others, it produces within them a thirst for more knowledge. Those are the people who can make new contributions to science that will continue to build upon the ever-broadening understanding of the stars and the universe.

Nicholas Copernicus

(1473–1543)

Nicholas Copernicus provided the first mathematical evidence in favor of a Sun-centered model of the universe. *(Photo courtesy of the Library of Congress)*

The Founder of Modern Astronomy

Nicholas Copernicus was a Polish astronomer and clergyman known as the founder of modern *astronomy*, since it was he who first introduced the *heliocentric* (Sun-centered) theory of the solar system in a way that others could comprehend. Before Copernicus, Europeans believed in the long-standing Ptolemaic system, which held that the Earth was the fixed center around which all other celestial objects orbited. It is remarkable that Copernicus was brave enough to propose a completely new astronomical theory. He lived during a time in civilized history when the Catholic Church governed much of Europe, and to suggest possibilities beyond what was accepted by the church as a known "truth," such as the Ptolemaic model of the solar system, was considered heresy—equivalent to denouncing God. The times, however, were changing. Ideas were beginning to be questioned. The Middle Ages were over, and Europe was in the middle of a social change called the Renaissance. Freethinking and deviation from the accepted scientific truths dictated by the early philosophers and upheld by the Catholic Church were slowly changing society. As an astronomical mathematician, Copernicus was chief among these revolutionary thinkers.

A Privileged Childhood

Copernicus lived a rather obscure life, the accounting of which has been told through bits and pieces of information gathered from scattered historical records. He was born Niclas Koppernigk in Torun, Poland, on February 19, 1473, into the privileged upper class. (Nicholas Copernicus is the Latinized form of his name.) His father, also Niclas Koppernigk, was a merchant who emigrated from Kraków, Poland, in about 1458. He became a successful businessman and magistrate in Torun. Nicholas's mother was Barbara Watzenrode, descended from generations of prosperous Torun merchants.

When Nicholas was 10 years old, his father died. His uncle, Lucas Watzenrode, a canon of Frauenburg Cathedral in Ermland, Prussia, took over the job of raising him and his three siblings. Nicholas first attended St. John's School in Torun and later the Cathedral School of Wloclawek, outside Torun.

In 1489 his uncle became the bishop of Ermland, which was the same as being its ruler. His uncle's high station was Nicholas's guarantee of a good education and bright future. In 1491, when Nicholas was 18, he traveled under the supervision of his uncle to the flourishing Polish city of Kraków to attend the University of Kraków. He looked forward to studying medicine, Latin, mathematics, astronomy, geography, philosophy, and, of course, church law, all subjects that would lead him toward a life of service to the church and a comfortable living for all of his days. Back then, as it is now, having a reliable income was no small thing.

Inspired to Study Astronomy

In the 15th century, science was not a university subject in and of itself, as it is today, but instead was part of the arts program. Astronomy was a subject taught mainly for the purpose of keeping a calendar, which enabled clergymen to keep track of spiritual holidays. One of the professors at the university was a Polish mathematician named Albert Brudzewski. There is no evidence that Copernicus actually attended his classes, but it is known that they were friends and that Brudzewski was key in introducing Nicholas to astronomy and inspiring in him a deep and lifelong interest in the subject. Brudzewski's astronomy was that of Ptolemy's, Aristotle's and, most important, the church's, which was the accepted, Earth-centered system.

Copernicus Recognizes a Need for Change

In the domain of the educated, Ptolemy's system, while largely unquestioned, had nevertheless always been regarded with a bit of quiet uncertainty. The universe, being that of the divine God, was considered to be perfect. A perfect God could create nothing less than a perfect universe. Thus, if the universe was perfect, why, then, did Ptolemy's system place the Earth off center? This was not perfection. It was cause for growing scandal among the scholars concerning the Earth-centered system, and it was inevitable that someone would eventually take genuine interest in setting things right. Copernicus was that person.

Over the past generations, observational techniques had slowly improved, and by this time it was known that when it came to predicting the seasons, Ptolemy's calendar was sometimes off by as much as a month. It disturbed Copernicus to know that if one were to employ Ptolemy's math, the Moon would have to change its size as it made its monthly revolutions in order to stay in keeping with Ptolemy's model. Such an inconsistency was unacceptable to him. This, together with a need to revise the current calendar, was cause for Copernicus to seek out a different, more perfect model for the construction of the universe. It was obvious that the true motions of

A Brief History of Accepted Astronomy

Theories of the early philosophers such as Aristotle (384–322 B.C.E.) and Ptolemy (ca. 87–150 C.E.) of an Earth-centered solar system (Ptolemaic system) were the accepted truths up until and during Copernicus's time. There were others before Copernicus, such as the

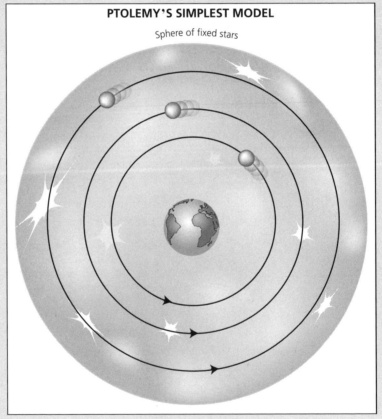

PTOLEMY'S SIMPLEST MODEL

Sphere of fixed stars

For the first, simplest model, Ptolemy described each planet orbiting the Earth with uniform circular motion contained within a sphere of fixed stars.

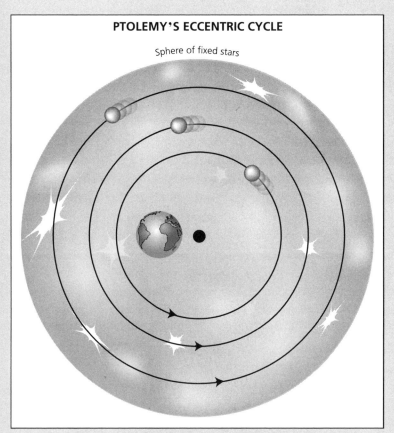

PTOLEMY'S ECCENTRIC CYCLE

Sphere of fixed stars

Ptolemy attempted to correct observed errors in the motions of the planets by modifying his simple Earth-centered system. He did this by placing the (fixed) Earth off-center while the planets remained orbiting the center with uniform circular motion. This system was not satisfactory either.

Greek philosopher Aristarchus of Samos (ca. 310–230 B.C.E.), who suggested the opposite: that the Earth revolved around the Sun. Lacking any real proof of this, however, Aristarchus's theory was rejected and Ptolemy's complex system stood for nearly 1,500 years. European civilization rested comfortably on the assumption that the

(continues)

(continued)

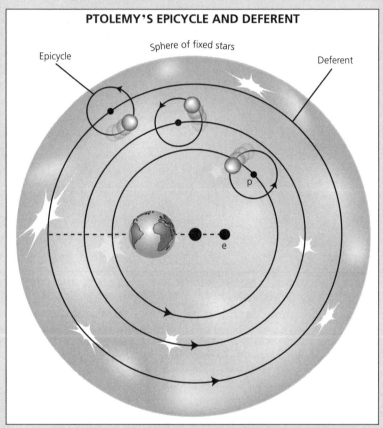

PTOLEMY'S EPICYCLE AND DEFERENT

Ptolemy added an epicycle, or small circle, to explain planetary retrograde motion. In the epicycle model, the planets orbit a center point (*p*) while the center travels around a larger circle, called a deferent, with the center offset from Earth. The equant point (*e*) is a location in space where calculations show that the planet would appear to be traveling uniformly.

Earth, not the Sun, was the fixed center of the universe and all celestial objects—the stars, planets, and the Sun—revolved around our stationary planet. Today this idea seems absurd, but during Copernicus's time it was considered the only truth. The Catholic Church had long ago accepted the Ptolemaic system as divine. It was the church's continued widespread influence along with human superstition that prevented the formal adoption of a heliocentric (Sun-centered) theory until the early 17th century.

When Ptolemy first began calculating the known motions of the planets and devising a model of the solar system that could be used to predict their positions in the future (and in that way predict the seasons), common sense placed the Earth in the center with all the stars, planets, and the Sun revolving around it. After all, was it not obvious that the Earth was standing still as everything in the heavens sailed past in circles? Thus, Ptolemy devised his first, perfectly balanced, Earth-centered system: the simplest of his systems.

This first straightforward system, however, did not account for the observed paths of the planets, which were known to make strange loops in the heavens called *retrograde* motion. Ptolemy could not force the math to work with the Earth at the center and still account for the planets' motions. He then tried putting the Earth off to the side of center, with the planets in an *eccentric* circle. This worked better, but still did not explain the quirky retrograde motions made by the planets.

Finally, in a brilliantly complex model, Ptolemy forced the Earth-centered system to work by employing his eccentric system and then applying individual motion to the planets, causing them to revolve around their own fixed center. This final system worked well enough to predict the planets' positions and gained acceptance as the working system of the universe. Ptolemy was not single-handedly responsible for devising the Earth-centered system, but he is usually given credit since it was he who made actual written recordings of the Earth-centered system in his book called the *Almagest* (Collection, ca. 140 C.E.).

the heavenly bodies were still not fully understood. When he started, he did not really intend to challenge Ptolemy's system, but rather rework the math until the system was perfect. Radical change, however, is exactly what Copernicus discovered was needed.

Observations and Calculations Begin

In 1496, after five years, Copernicus's uncle moved him from the University of Kraków to the University of Bologna, Italy, in order for him to study canon law, or church law. The next year he received an official notice that his uncle had secured for him a canonry position at Frauenburg Cathedral, Ermland, which would provide him ample income without his having to return and perform any duties in person. He could stay in Italy and continue his studies. This was fine with him, for in Bologna he could continue to study astronomy and work on Ptolemy's calculations.

Copernicus was not a celestial observationist, but instead more of an applied mathematics astronomer, doing his astronomical calculations alone in a candlelit room. He did finally begin making and recording his own observations from the roof of astronomy professor Domenico Maria de Novara's home. On March 9, 1497, he recorded the observation of the Moon eclipsing the star Aldeberan. Aside from conducting observations, he also began studying all of the known theories of the solar system. He explored the observations and mathematical hypotheses of, not just Ptolemy and Aristotle, but the theories of the Greek mathematician Aristarchus (310–230 B.C.E.) and the Greek philosopher Philolaus (b. ca. 475 B.C.E.) as well, the latter two having long ago proposed the radical idea that the Sun, and not the Earth, stood at the center of the universe.

In 1500, Copernicus visited Rome, where he gave lectures on mathematics and observed a lunar *eclipse*. He stayed for close to one year. Then he traveled to Frauenburg, where, in 1501, he was officially inaugurated as a canon of the Ermland Chapter. Shortly afterward, he set out for the University of Padua in Rome to study medicine and also to continue his studies in astronomy in his free time. By 1503, he relocated yet again, this time to the University of Ferrara, where he finally received his doctorate in canon law. He then moved back to Padua to finish his education in medicine. By

1506, war had broken out, and Copernicus decided to move back to Ermland.

The Heliocentric System Marks a Scientific Revolution

Rather than take up his duties as canon to Frauenburg Cathedral, he instead became medical adviser and secretary to his uncle Lucas Watzenrode, who was beginning to age. Copernicus took up residence with him in his castle at Heilsberg, about 40 miles (64 km) southeast of Frauenburg. For the next six years, Copernicus helped manage his uncle's duties, yet during all this time he also worked on geometric celestial calculations, writing down his findings, calculating and recalculating until eventually he devised a beautifully simple mathematical system, one in which he placed the Sun at the center of the universe. Copernicus had worked out the correct model of the solar system. The problem was that it was not the church-accepted model. Copernicus knew his calculations were right, yet he did not seek to advertise his findings for fear of being labeled a heretic.

By 1512, Copernicus had completed a brief outline of his new theory titled *Commentariolus* (Little commentary). Since it flew in the face of church doctrine, he did not publish this work but instead circulated handwritten, unsigned copies among trusted colleagues. According to a University of Saint Andrew history article titled "Nicholas Copernicus" written by J. J. O'Connor and E. F. Robertson, the book consisted of seven principles, or laws:

- There is no one center in the universe.
- The Earth's center is not the center of the universe.
- The center of the solar system is near the Sun.
- The distance from the Earth to the Sun is imperceptible compared with the distance to the stars.
- The rotation of the Earth accounts for the apparent daily rotation of the stars.
- The apparent annual cycle of movements of the Sun is caused by the Earth revolving round it.
- The apparent retrograde motion of the planets is caused by the motion of the Earth, from which one observes.

Commentariolus was merely Copernicus's brief outline for what would someday become a major volume, the book for which he is most famous: *De revolutionibus orbium coelestium* (On the revolutions of the celestial orbits), published in 1543.

It was in 1512 also that his uncle died, a great turning point in Copernicus's life, for his uncle had always been his cornerstone. Copernicus was now left to manage life on his own. Within the year, he returned to Frauenburg Cathedral as canon and took up residence in one of its turrets, which served as his observatory.

During his stay at Frauenburg, Copernicus committed to writing his great book, *De revolutionibus orbium coelestium*, which describes in mathematical detail his heliocentric theory. But he was a very busy man and years would pass before the manuscript was ready for publication. In 1516, he was appointed administrator of two of the outlying estates, Allenstien and Mehlsack, and thus moved to Allenstien Castle. Due to war brewing between Prussia's Teutonic knights and Poland, by 1519 he was again back at Frauenburg. Protected behind the fortifications of the cathedral walls, he continued his celestial observations for the next year and made revisions on his now massive *De revolutionibus*.

The year 1521 saw an end to the war and also Copernicus's appointment as commissar of Ermland. For the next several years, Copernicus devoted much of his time to putting Ermland financially back together. A close friend of his named Tiedemann Giese, who was another canon in the chapter, assisted him. Copernicus was aware of the importance behind the exchange of money for goods and became deeply involved in the economic difficulties that arose after the war.

The Religious Scandal

Throughout the late 1520s and early 1530s, Copernicus's duties of state gradually passed to other men. His manuscript *De revolutionibus* had seen many revisions but never a publisher. By now, Copernicus had earned a reputation as being quite a good physician, yet he became more reclusive and socially out of touch. Most of his friends and family had died. His beloved Catholic Church now knew about and was criticizing his stand on the heliocentric theory of the solar system. Even the Protestants, the Catholic Church's opponents, had learned of and criticized his views. Educated men, such as the German theologian Martin Luther, founder of the Protestant religion, and Philip Melanchthon, another German theologian, publicly denounced Copernicus, which caused his "heretical teachings" to be known by everyone, not just the broad inner circle of scholars. Commoners suddenly became involved in the scandal, even devising a stage play intended to mock his theory.

The situation was not completely lost for Copernicus, however. Here and there, men cropped up who were open to his teachings. For instance, in 1533, a papal officer named John Widmanstad gave a supportive speech about the new theory to the Pope Clement VII and a few cardinals. In 1536, Cardinal Nicholas von Schönberg appealed to Copernicus in a letter he posted from Rome, pleading with him to publish his manuscript. Copernicus would not.

Throughout all the scandal, Copernicus continued to practice medicine. He was gaining renown as a physician, rather than as an astronomer. He was frequently called upon to attend the ailing Mauritius Ferber, who was appointed as the new bishop of Ermland in 1523. It was an honor to be entrusted with the medical care of such an important person. Copernicus also served as physician for Dantiscus, the bishop who succeeded Ferber in 1538. Even Duke Albert of Prussia sent for Copernicus to administer to his personal counselor Georg von Kunheim, who had fallen suddenly and gravely ill. Copernicus succeeded in nursing the sick man back to health, a feat that no previous physician had accomplished.

Copernicus's Legacy

In 1539, a young mathematician arrived at Frauenburg unannounced. His name was Georg Joachim, but he is known simply as Rheticus, which means "the man from Rhaetia," the European city in which he was born. His purpose was to discover from Copernicus more information about this new astronomical system he had heard about. Rheticus, it turned out, was a professor of mathematics from the University of Wittenberg, a purely Protestant community.

Since Rheticus was a Protestant, Copernicus had every right as a devout Catholic not to receive him, but instead he welcomed him. Rheticus set to work studying Copernicus's manuscript, which was in its final stages of completion. After a few months, Rheticus had reproduced the basics of the theory in a little book he called *First Account*, which he sent to his former professor Johann Schöner. With Copernicus's permission, it was published in 1540.

Because of Rheticus, his encouragement, and the publication of *First Account*, Copernicus finally agreed to publish his remarkable work, *De revolutionibus*. In the first pages of the book, Copernicus included the 1536 letter from Nicholas von Schönberg, the Roman Catholic cardinal who had implored him to publish his theory. The rest of the book dealt with his heliocentric model of the solar system and his Sun-centered mathematical calculations that adequately complemented the looping paths performed by the planets.

The book provided many reasons why it was logical for the Sun to exist at the center of the solar system. For instance, the predictions of planetary locations matched the observations that were in existence. Also, with this new system the Moon's apparent size did not have to change, and the astronomical models were no longer off center, this last of which was the most objectionable concept of the Ptolemaic system. It also greatly improved the accuracy of the calendar.

Rheticus took charge of the duties involved in publishing the manuscript and had it sent to a man in Nuremberg named John Petrijus. His involvement came to an end, however, when he was suddenly offered a position at Leipzig University. Rheticus handed the duties of overseeing the publication to a Protestant preacher named Andrew Osiander.

Then, late in 1542, Copernicus had a stroke. He survived, but suffered from apoplexy, a form of partial paralysis. A competent physician, Vicar Fabian Emmerich, attended him, but he was not expected to live long.

Osiander, whose job it now was to publish Copernicus's book, was very concerned about the content of *De revolutionibus* and how it conflicted with the church's long-established model of the solar system. Copernicus was in no condition to object, so before the book went to press, Osiander took it upon himself to write his own

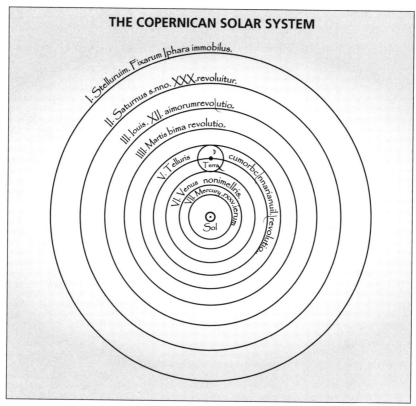

A reproduction of Copernicus's diagram of the solar system from Book One of
De revolutionibus orbium coelestium (On the revolutions of the celestial orbits)

foreword. For years, readers assumed that Copernicus himself had
written the foreword.

George Abell states in his book *Exploration of the Universe* (1969),
"Osiander wrote a preface, which he neglected to sign, expressing
the (modern) view that the science presented only an abstract
mathematical hypothesis, and implying that the theory set forth in
the book was only a convenient calculating scheme."

Years later, the German astronomer Johannes Kepler (1571–
1630) finally revealed to the public that the true author of the foreword was not Copernicus but Andrew Osiander.

In May 1543, while Copernicus lay on his deathbed, weakened
in mind and body, he was handed the first printed copy of *De revolutionibus orbium coelestium*. A short while later, he died of a brain

hemorrhage. Throughout his career, most of his peers considered his theory implausible, but to his own credit the mathematician stood behind his work to the very end. An excerpt from *De revolutionibus orbium coelestium* reads:

> Finally we shall place the Sun himself at the center of the Universe. All this is suggested by the systematic procession of events and the harmony of the whole universe, if only we face the facts, as they say, "with both eyes open."

Although his system still had its problems, such as the idea that all bodies moved in perfect circles (which they do not) and that a sphere of fixed stars surrounded the solar system, today's modern astronomy is based on the Copernican system. Not only did this brave and quiet man provide humankind with the means of understanding the structure of the universe, but he also taught scientists to keep an open mind and never make the mistake of ruling anything out when it comes to making new discoveries.

CHRONOLOGY

1473	Born Niclas Koppernigk on February 19 in Torun, Poland
1491	Enters the University of Kraków and is inspired to study astronomy
1496	Begins to study canon law at the University of Bologna, Italy
1497	Receives a canonry at the cathedral in Frauenburg (now Frombork), Poland, allowing him freedom to continue his astronomical work
1500	Observes a lunar eclipse while visiting Rome
1501	Moves to the University of Padua, Italy, to study medicine
1503	Receives a doctorate in canon law from the University of Ferrara, Italy
1506–12	Acts as secretary and medical adviser to his uncle Lucas Watzenrode

1516	Appointed administrator of two of the outlying estates, Allenstien and Mehlsack
1519	Moves back to Frauenburg Cathedral and resumes studies in astronomy
1539	Convinced by German mathematician Rheticus to publish *De revolutionibus orbium coelestium* (On the revolutions of the celestial orbits)
1542	Rendered helpless by a stroke
1543	His life work, *De revolutionibus orbium coelestium,* is published, including an unauthorized foreword written by Andrew Osiander; Copernicus dies on May 24 in Frauenburg, Poland

FURTHER READING

Books

Andronik, Catherine M. *Copernicus: Founder of Modern Astronomy (Great Minds of Science).* Berkeley Heights, N.J.: Enslow Publishers, 2002. An excellent, well-organized, and illustrated account of the contributions Copernicus made toward the development of astronomy.

Armitage, Angus. *The World of Copernicus.* New York: Signet, 1947. A nicely researched classic about Copernicus and his struggle to introduce change to the scientific world.

Copernicus, Nicholas. *De revolutionibus orbium coelestium* (CD-ROM). Oakland, Calif.: Octavo Corporation, 1999. A CD-ROM of Copernicus's edition originally published in Nuremberg, 1543. Contains each page of the treatise and the binding, photographed at very high resolution. Adobe PDF file includes software to view, search, and print.

Goble, Todd, and William J. Boerst. *Nicolaus Copernicus and the Founding of Modern Astronomy (Great Scientists).* Greensboro, N.C.: Morgan Reynolds, 2003. Tailored toward students in grades 6–8, this is a methodical biography of Nicholas Copernicus addressing the religious turmoil and political unrest of his times as he dared to challenge the medieval astronomical theories with his modern heliocentric model of the solar system.

Kuhn, Thomas S. *The Copernican Revolution.* Cambridge, Mass.: Harvard University Press, 1992. A condensed and well-written book on the achievements of Copernicus. The author investigates the cresting theory of Copernicanism and its effects on the other sciences.

Web Sites

The About Network. "Profiles in Courage: Copernicus." Available online. URL: http://atheism.miningco.com/library/weekly/aa101 498.htm?terms=copernicus&COB=home. Accessed November 29, 2004. A 1,000-word biography provided by the About Network profiling Copernicus's accomplishments and their association and conflict with European religious dogma of the time.

2

Tycho Brahe

(1546–1601)

Tycho Brahe developed superior observational techniques to study celestial objects. (*Photo courtesy of the Library of Congress*)

The Astronomer Who Revolutionized Techniques of Celestial Observation

Tycho Brahe was a Danish astronomer who grew to become such an excellent celestial observer that King Frederick II of Denmark gave him the entire island of Hven, off the coast of Denmark, on which to build what became the finest observatory in all Europe during that time: the castle observatory of Uraniborg. His lifetime of observations was made just before the invention of the telescope;

17

therefore, he used only his naked eye and precision instruments of his own creation to measure positions of the stars and planets in the night sky.

Born into Privilege

Raised as an only child, Tycho (pronounced "teeko," as it is in Latin) Brahe was born Tyge Brahe on December 14, 1546, at Knutstorps Castle in Skaane, Denmark (now in Sweden) as a twin. His twin, Niels Brahe, died at birth. Tycho was the firstborn son to his father, Otte Brahe, a distinguished nobleman who was governor of Helsingborg Castle and member of the Danish Rigsraad (elevated in 1563). The Rigsraad, or Council of the Realm, was made up of about 20 members whose courtly duties included appointing regents, declaring war and peace, seating kings and then advising them on nearly every matter. His mother, Beate Bille, was also of noble decent.

Tycho Brahe had strange (but not unusual for the time) circumstances surrounding his birth. His parents agreed before he was born to allow his adoption by Otte's brother, Jorgen Brahe, and his wife, Ingar Oxe, who were childless. When Tycho was born, however, his father changed his mind. This angered Jorgen and Ingar, for they had been promised a son. Two years later, Jorgen kidnapped Tycho. This infuriated Otte, but the brothers soon came to an agreement when Jorgen pointed out that Tycho would live like a prince, be well educated, and someday inherit Jorgen's estate. Otte agreed and Tycho became "nephew" to his own father and mother.

Lunar Eclipse Shifts His Educational Goal toward Astronomy

When Tycho was seven years old, he began his schooling at a clerical school near Vordingborg, where he received his elementary education and learned the Latin language, both spoken and written. In 1559, at age 13, Tycho began classical studies at the University of Copenhagen, and, although he focused on law, the university offered education in astronomy and the mathematics that accompany its study. This is where Brahe became deeply involved in the subject. It was within the first year at Copenhagen that he discovered through one of his professors a basic pre-Copernican astronomy book by English mathematician and astronomer Johannes de Sacrobosco (d. ca. 1256) titled *De sphaera* (On the spheres, ca. 1230). Then, on August 21, 1560, Brahe experienced a life-altering event by witnessing a partial eclipse of the Sun. It was not the phenomenon of the eclipse itself, however, that fascinated him. It was the fact that its occurrence had been predicted beforehand. To Brahe, this was amazing! That people could predict the movements of the planets was a feat of mathematical genius that he wanted to be able to carry out for himself.

Brahe had the benefit of family wealth and thus had the resources to supply himself with the tools required to follow his heart. He never advertised his passion for astronomy to members of his household, for he suspected that they would disapprove. Cautiously, he began purchasing his own copies of more advanced astronomy books. He also acquired an *ephemeris* of planetary motions, which is a table that gives the positions of the stars and planets over a time period. Privately, he set about learning all that he could about astronomy.

A Need for Change in Observational Accuracy

In 1562, after three years in Copenhagen, Brahe left for the University of Leipzig, in Germany, with a personal tutor named Anders Sorensen Vedel (who later became a famous Danish historian). At Leipzig, Brahe continued his classical studies under the directions of his tutor. When Vedel was not around, however, he remained faithful to his study of astronomy. As time passed and he became more familiar with the heavens, Brahe was able to locate and name all the constellations. He began to keep track of the movements of the planets. Upon comparing his data with that of Ptolemy, whose predictions were sometimes off by as much as a month, and Copernicus, whose predictions could be off by days, Brahe realized that there was still a tremendous amount of work to be done in terms of accurate predictions.

No longer willing to keep his love of astronomy secret, he decided to take a first step away from the education that had been chosen for him. Brahe did this by enrolling in an *astrology* course. It was not long before he began to formulate horoscopes for important men. He also began a notebook on celestial observations, the first of what would become many of his observation logs. His goal was to work out the most accurate planetary predictions that had ever been. He began this first log in late summer 1563.

His studies in law began to suffer as his interest in a life dedicated to the study of astronomy surfaced. His tutor tried to keep the now 17-year-old boy on task, but it was of no use. Brahe was headstrong, and astronomy was in his blood. Finally, the tutor gave up, saying Brahe was a hopeless case; yet despite this rift, they remained friends their whole lives.

Design Begins on Observational Instruments

In the pursuit of astronomy, Brahe became very familiar with the many subjects with which it is closely associated, such as mathematics, cartography, geography, navigation, and the use and construction of observational instruments. Brahe's first instrument used for observation was a cross-staff, or astronomical radius. It soon became clear that he was in need of a better instrument. Thus Brahe set about designing his first astronomical instrument for measuring the stellar positions.

In 1565, Brahe left Leipzig for Denmark, which was currently at war with Sweden. At this time, his uncle Jorgen, a vice admiral, was in Copenhagen with his fleet when King Fredrik II fell from his own boat into the waters surrounding the royal castle. While trying to rescue the king, Jorgen fell in after him and died a short while later from pneumonia contracted from the ordeal.

After his uncle Jorgen's death, Brahe spent a year in Denmark with his natural family, included now as brother and son instead of cousin and nephew. The only family member who supported his love for astronomy was another uncle, Steen Bille. Seeing no sense in staying where his family would constantly nag him about his future, Brahe was soon off to Rostok, Germany, where he entered the university.

For the next four years, Brahe continued his education, moving from Rostok to Augsburg. In Augsburg, during spring 1570, he finished construction on his famous Great Quadrant, the largest instrument of its kind both then and now. It was 18 feet (5.5 m) in diameter and made entirely from oak, except for the brass graduation strip and plumb bob, and turned on four great handles (see page 23). It was so heavy and cumbersome that 40 men were needed to install it!

For two months, Brahe made weekly observations

TYCHO'S FIRST INSTRUMENT

Tycho Brahe's first self-designed instrument for measuring stellar positions was finished in 1569.

with it, recording his findings, making adjustments, and exhausting his servants with the amount of work it took to handle it. Rumor spread, and due to the Great Quadrant, Brahe began to make a name for himself as a serious astronomer rather than merely an astrological forecaster. The Great Quadrant was only the first of all the fascinating instruments he would design in order to observe the stars and planets, for there is one important thing he discovered that would change the practice of astronomical science forever: astronomy needed accurate and constant—not occasional—observational data.

In winter 1570, Brahe left Germany and returned home to the family's Knundstrup Castle to attend at the deathbed of his father, Otte, who later died in May 1571. He also met and grew to love a common woman by the name of Kirsten Barbara Jorgensdatter. Due to their differing social status—he a noble and she a commoner—they were not allowed to marry in the eyes of the Catholic Church.

Tycho Brahe's Metal Nose

There is another matter regarding Brahe's fame, and that is his metal nose! In 1566, during a Christmas celebration in Rostok, Brahe became quarrelsome with another Danish student named Manderup Parsberg. It is not clear exactly what the argument was about, but it was likely over mathematics or the validity of one or two of Brahe's recent astronomical predictions. The two men ended up in a duel with swords (duels were common among European nobility, frequently resulting in death). The fight ended when Brahe was slashed across the face and a section of his nose severed off. He spent long days recuperating from his wound. Later, the young astronomer had a false nosepiece made to hide his disfigurement. Most accounts state the nosepiece was made from gold or a mix of silver and gold, and held in place using an adhesive salve. However, in 1901, on the 300th anniversary of his death, Brahe was exhumed, or taken from his grave, for the purposes of determining whether or not his body was in there. Indeed, there was the body with a disfigured nose (as well as the body of a woman who is presumed to be his common-law wife, Kirsten). Around the nose area, traces of green were found on the scar tissue, indicative that perhaps the nosepiece was made of copper. Alternatively, he may have had a "formal" nosepiece of gold and then another lighter copper version for daily wear. Some of his portraits clearly show the false nose.

Despite this, they lived together all their lives, and Kirsten gave birth to three sons and five daughters. (Unions between nobles and commoners were discouraged, but were not out of the ordinary and were viewed as common-law marriages.)

After his father's death, Brahe moved to nearby Herrevad Abbey to live with his maternal uncle Steen Bille, the only relative who approved of his devotion to astronomy and of his more

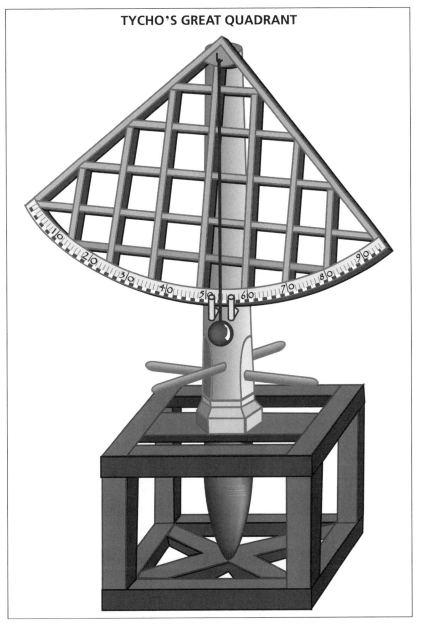

TYCHO'S GREAT QUADRANT

Tycho Brahe designed and built his Great Quadrant in 1570 in Augsburg, Germany.

recent scientific interest, chemistry. Steen Bille was responsible for building the first paper mill and glassworks in Denmark, and he dabbled in alchemy (chemical research) as well, so he had his own laboratory in which to conduct experiments. The two had enough in common for them to get along quite well together.

His Discoveries on the Supernova of 1572

It was at Herrevad Abbey on November 11, 1572, while Brahe was walking from his uncle's alchemy laboratory to the main house, that an event happened that would change his life, elevating him to royal astronomer and master over the finest observatory ever built in Europe. Looking up to the heavens that night, Brahe noticed within the constellation Cassiopeia a bright new star, one that had never been there before. This was not possible! The stars did not change within the eighth sphere of unchangeable heavens, not now, not in the beginning of creation, nor for eternity to come!

Unable to believe his eyes, Brahe called together servants and passing peasants to bear witness to this new star, a supernova that shone more brightly than Jupiter's closest approach. Brahe had to determine exactly what this new object was. Laying aside his chemistry work, he settled into his observations using his newest instrument, a grand sextant with arms five and one-half feet (1.68 m) long, marked to the minute, and accompanied by a table of corrections he had compiled in order to account for any error that the instrument might invite. After a few nights of careful observation, he was soon convinced that the bright object was undeniably a star, not a comet or a planet, for it did not possess a filmy tail or move in any way relative to the other stars. Therefore, he concluded, it must indeed exist in the eighth sphere, the boundary of fixed stars whose divine unchangeability was held in relationship with the perfection of God himself. This shattered the Catholic views declaring that only within the boundary between the Earth and Moon—the sublunary sphere—did things change. No one had seen or recorded anything such as this. (Hipparchus, around 125 B.C.E., was the only other person to see and describe the appearance of a new star.) Brahe's supernova burned for 18 months before gradually fading

The First Observation of a Supernova

In about 125 B.C.E., the Greek astronomer, geographer, and mathematician Hipparchus observed a supernova, *nova* meaning "new star." (Of course, it is now known that a supernova is an exploding star, thus a dying star, not a "new star"). This event caused him to want to discover if stars were born and then died. He also created his own star catalog of close to 1,000 stars, in which he divides stars into classes according to their brightness, called *magnitude*. His catalog was used for the next 1,600 years, and his system of measuring brightness is still employed today. He is also responsible for discovering that the Earth wobbles slightly on its axis; he estimated the size of the Moon and its distance from Earth; he formulated a method for predicting eclipses; he calculated the length of the year to within six and one-half minutes, and discovered the *precession of equinoxes*.

into oblivion, but at its height of brilliance it was sometimes visible even during the day.

The Book *De nove stella* Gains Him Fame

In 1573, Brahe published his first book *De nove et nullius aevi memoria prius visa stella* (On the new and never previously seen star), more commonly known as *De nove stella* (The new star). This book contained a variety of subjects, from astrological predictions to calendars, but most important, a 27-page detailed description of the new star, an object whose existence produced first-time evidence that challenged without question the previously assumed fixed nature of the heavens. *De nove stella* made Brahe famous throughout Europe.

Ready to enjoy his new fame, Brahe began to travel, giving lectures and visiting with other astronomers. By 1575, he found himself at Cassel, Germany, as a guest of the ruling Count Wilhelm IV of Hesse, who for the past 20 years was actively involved in astronomy and had on his grounds an observatory complete with his own astronomical instruments of observation.

Europe's First Astronomical Research Facility Is Built on Hven Island

Word spread to the Danish king Frederick regarding Brahe's achievements in astronomy; however, it seemed Brahe had plans to move to Basle, Germany, and not home to Denmark. As a Danish noble, King Frederick expected Brahe to return to Denmark and serve his own country as a royal astronomer. He offered Brahe a number of different castles, but Brahe refused them, stating that the duties associated with the governing of such castles would interfere with his work in astronomy. King Frederick sent desperate notice that the island of Hven off the Danish coast would be a nicely isolated location on which to build the royal observatory, and he would very much like Brahe to accept this offer to become the first professional astronomer to Denmark. Brahe agreed, and in 1576 he received the island of Hven with the promise to have built for him a grand observatory, an estate in which to live, and the island's villagers and farmers to serve as his subjects.

Brahe hired a German architect to construct an observatory the likes of which had never been seen. He named it Uraniborg after Urania, the goddess of the sky. It was ornately detailed with a great onion dome, a surrounding 250-foot (76.2 m) wall, extensive gardens, a basement for alchemy, a dungeon for miscreants, and a paper mill and printing press. Huge rooms housed his astronomical equipment. From Augsburg he commissioned a brass globe, five feet (1.5 m) in diameter, that sat within the library and received engravings of the stars as his observations described them. He employed a large staff, instruments, and timepieces with which to make as many as four simultaneous measurements of the same

Tycho Brahe's famous underground observatory, Stjerneborg, was destroyed sometime after his death. A replica has been constructed on Hven Island according to Brahe's surviving diagrams. *(Photo by Larry Adkins)*

object. Uraniborg was an astronomer's dream. It was also the perfect place to invite guests, and Brahe loved parties. He would entertain them with feasts and oddities such as a dwarf soothsayer and a tame moose.

Later, Brahe added a second observatory he called Stjerneborg, or Starry Castle. Except for the domed roofs, the building existed completely underground in order to help protect the observational instruments from the damaging effects of wind and vibration. Brahe devised a clever system of communication for both buildings, a system of bells he could ring to summon servants from any room to his location.

The Distant Comet and the Tychonic System

In November 1577, Brahe had another unusual experience, similar to that of the 1572 supernova. A comet appeared in the night sky. This excited him very much, and he began new observations. After using *parallax* measurements, he came to the astonishing conclusion that the object existed farther away than the Moon. Again, this was more evidence against the established theories that only within the sublunary sphere did things move and change. Until Brahe and his instruments came along, comets were accepted as burning gases in the *atmosphere* of Earth. His observations disproved this theory and the theory that each planet rode on its own transparent sphere through which "atmospheric" comets could never pass. Like the supernova, the comet showed that the unchangeable sphere of fixed

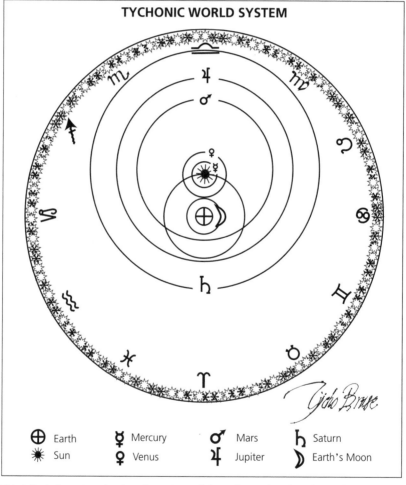

This is Brahe's system showing the 12 signs of the zodiac within the sphere of fixed stars. Brahe believed the Earth was the stationary center of the universe, with the Sun orbiting the Earth and the known planets circling the Sun.

stars indeed experienced change. Eleven years after observing the comet he published a book on his findings called *De mundi aetherei recentioribus phoenomenis liber secundus* (About recently viewed phenomena in the ether sphere, 1588).

After the comet experience, Brahe put great effort into trying to determine parallax motion in the stars. When he found there were none, his calculations brought him to two conclusions: either the Earth was the fixed center of the universe (not the Sun, as the newly introduced Copernican system showed), or the stars were too far away to show parallax motion. Forced to choose between them, he resolved that the stars could not possibly be that far away, so he decided against Copernican theory. He eventually developed his own planetary model, which could be described as half heliocentric and half *geocentric*. That is to say, he placed the planets in circular motion around the Sun, but then he placed the Sun and planets in circular motion around a fixed Earth. Naturally, he labeled this new system the Tychonic system, but his system was in fact very similar to one modeled by the Greek philosopher and astronomer Heracleides of Pontus (b. ca. 388 B.C.E.). Brahe's system never became popular.

Brahe's Legacy

During his years at Uraniborg, Brahe accomplished a great amount of work. He established entirely new methods for celestial observation and compiled a star catalog. He designed and constructed a wide range of astronomical instruments with which to record his measurements, some that were accurate to within four minutes of an *arc* (1/15 of a degree), and he was the first to compensate for atmospheric refraction. His logs and publications (many printed on his own press) would become the stepping-stones for future astronomers.

As the years passed, Brahe grew increasingly arrogant and ill tempered. He commonly locked his servants in chains and made unreasonable demands on his island subjects. His manner was gruff and his attitude unbearable. Once the pride of Denmark, Brahe was now despised by many Danes. After his friend King Frederick died of alcohol poisoning in 1588, the new king, Christian IV, began to send letters to Brahe addressing his ill-treatment of his subjects, letters that Brahe left unanswered. King Christian responded to

Brahe's egotism by limiting his income until finally, in 1597, Brahe left Uraniborg.

Unwelcome in Denmark, he and his entourage of family, servants, instruments, and manuscripts took to traveling. In 1598, in Wandsburg, Germany, Tycho published a book he had started at Uraniborg titled *Astronomiae instauratae mechanica* (The new astronomy's instrumentology) containing his autobiography and descriptions and pictures of his instruments and buildings on Hven. Finally, in 1599, Brahe moved to Prague to take the seat as chief mathematician and astronomer to Emperor Rudolph II, who loved anything to do with astrology, mysticism, and the secrets of the universe. The emperor offered Brahe a castle and an income of such worth it caused unrest with the nobles who had served the court for years and did not make nearly as much as this new Danish "fortune-teller," a name often used to refer to astrologers.

Eventually settling within the city, in 1600 Brahe hired a skilled assistant, young Johannes Kepler, to help him with the emperor's commission: compiling a new set of astronomical tables based on Brahe's nearly 40 years of observational data. Although the two of them disagreed on the mechanics of the solar system (Kepler was a devout believer in the new Copernican system, whereas Brahe was not), they otherwise related well enough to work together, even though Brahe kept many of his observational methods and data secret from Kepler.

The next year, 1601, was Brahe's last. While he attended a dinner at the estate of his friend Peter Vok Ursinus Rozmberk, it is said that, adhering to court etiquette, Brahe refrained from leaving the table before his host even while he was suffering from an overfull bladder. This caused him great physical distress. After he returned home that evening, matters became worse and he could only pass urine a little at a time and under terrible pain. Eleven days later, on October 24, 1601, he died in excruciating pain.

In 1602, Kepler finished and published Brahe's *Astronomiae instauratae progymnasmata* (Introduction to the new astronomy). This book established the observational and theoretical techniques that launched a new era of modern astronomy.

Brahe's precise cause of death was never determined, yet many assumed that Brahe died from complications resulting from the holding of his urine. In 1991, however, the director of the Czech National Museum gave the Danish government a box containing a bit of shroud and some remnants of beard belonging to Brahe, which had been taken from the tomb during the 1901 exhumation. Analysis of the beard hairs showed an unusually high concentration of mercury. Some poisonings from heavy metals match uremia-like symptoms (urine in the blood), which describes the death of Brahe. With this new evidence, some experts today believe Brahe died from mercury poisoning.

Brahe's tomb resides at the Tyn church in Prague, yet his fantastic instruments are lost to the ages. Uraniborg and Stjerneborg have long been destroyed, but the work that took place there endures. Brahe's lifetime of recorded observations passed to Johannes Kepler and greatly assisted in his formulation of his three laws of planetary motion.

Brahe's accomplishments played a highly significant role in the development of modern astronomy and the way humans view the world and the universe. He created a remarkably accurate star catalog of approximately 1,000 stars, proved that comets were not objects in the atmosphere but instead existed beyond the Moon, and made overall improvements on the known methods of observation.

CHRONOLOGY

1546	Born as Tyge Brahe on December 14 in Skane, Denmark (now Sweden)
1548	Goes to live with his uncle Jorgen Brahe
1559	Enters the University of Copenhagen to study philosophy and law
1560	Witnesses a partial eclipse of the Sun and becomes interested in astronomy
1562	Enters the University of Leipzig, Germany
1563	Begins his first observational log
1565	Leaves Leipzig for Denmark. Jorgen Brahe dies of pneumonia.

1566	Travels to Rostok, Germany, to attend the university; loses part of his nose in a duel with another student
1570	Finishes construction on his famous Great Quadrant
1571	Returns to Denmark and meets his future life partner, Kirsten Jorgensdatter. His father, Otte, dies in May.
1572	Discovers a new star, a supernova, within the constellation Cassiopeia
1573	Publishes his famous book *De nove stella* (The new star)
1576	Is presented with Hven Island by King Frederick II; the castle observatory Uraniborg is built
1577	Observes and records the path of a comet and proves it existed beyond the Moon
1588	Publishes *De mundi aetherei recentioribus phoenomenis liber secundus* (About recently viewed phenomena in the ether sphere). King Frederick II dies of alcohol poisoning.
1597	Funding is cut off by King Christian IV, forcing him to depart from Uraniborg forever
1598	Publishes *Astronomiae instauratae mechanica* (The new astronomy's instrumentology)
1599	Becomes chief astronomer to Emperor Rudolph II of Prague
1600	Hires Johannes Kepler as an assistant
1601	Dies on October 24 of what is now thought to be mercury poisoning
1602	Johannes Kepler finishes and then publishes Brahe's *Astronomiae instauratae progymnasmata* (Introduction to the new astronomy)

FURTHER READING

Books

Boerst, William J. *Tycho Brahe: Mapping the Heavens (Great Scientists)*. Greensboro, N.C.: Morgan Reynolds, 2002. From

Boerst's *Great Scientists* collection, a study designed for students in grades 6–12 on the life of Tycho Brahe and his accomplishments in science.

Christianson, John R. *On Brahe's Island: Tycho Brahe and His Assistants, 1570–1601*. Cambridge: Cambridge University Press, 1999. A vivid portrayal of life at Uraniborg and the people who contributed to Europe's first scientific research center.

Dreyer, J. L. E. *Tycho Brahe: A Picture of Scientific Life and Work in the Sixteenth Century*. Edinburgh: Adam & Charles Black, 1890. Reprint, New York: Dover, 1963. A systematic, well-done study on Tycho Brahe and his work.

Gow, Mary. *Tycho Brahe: Astronomer (Great Minds of Science)*. Berkeley Heights, N.J.: Enslow Publishers, 2002. Tailored toward readers in grades 6–10, the book illustrates Brahe's life in easy-to-follow language.

Thoren, Victor E. *The Lord of Uraniborg: A Biography of Tycho Brahe*. Cambridge: Cambridge University Press, 1990. This is an engaging, concise biography of Tycho Brahe that explores every aspect of his life and his life's work.

Web Sites

Tycho Brahe Homepage. Available online. URL: http://www.nada. kth.se/~fred/tycho. Accessed November 29, 2004. A Web site dedicated to Tycho Brahe and his accomplishments in astronomy. Includes portraits, a biography, and links to other sites.

Runeberg, John. "Tycho Brahe's Castle Uraniborg and His Observatory Stjärneborg." Available online. URL: http://www. hven.net/EUBORG.html. Accessed November 29, 2004. Johan Runeberg hosts this Web site that offers detailed information and drawings of Tycho Brahe's Uraniborg Castle and his underground observatory, Stjärneborg. Also offers links to more Tycho Brahe and Hven Island information.

3

Galileo Galilei

(1564–1642)

Galileo revolutionized 16th-century European astronomy by greatly improving on the first crude telescope designs by Dutch lens maker Jan Lippershey. *(Photo courtesy of the Library of Congress)*

Physicist Revolutionizes Astronomical Observation with the Newly Invented Telescope

Among history's early astronomers, Galileo is famous mainly for his use of the first telescope directed into the night sky. He is celebrated as a physical scientist and as a supporter of the heliocentric solar system, or Copernicanism, as it was known in his time. By improving the original telescope designs of Jan Lippershey (1570–1619), a lens maker from the Netherlands, Galileo used observations and mathematics to revolutionize the scientific scene in Europe by providing overwhelming proof that the 1,500-year-old Ptolemaic (Earth-centered) model of the universe was wrong. He is also known as the first person to discover the four large moons of Jupiter.

Born in Pisa

Galileo Galilei was born on February 15, 1564 in Pisa, Italy, to Vincenzio Galilei, a musician, math tutor, and merchant descended from a Florentine patrician family, and Giulia degli Ammannati, an aristocratic woman from Pescia.

In 1574, the family moved to Florence and Galileo began studies at the Camaldolese Monastery at Vallombrosa. He found he liked the lifestyle of the monks, and in 1578 he officially entered the order as a novice, announcing that he would like to join when he was old enough. His father forbade it and informed Galileo, who was a bright pupil, that he was to study to become a physician, which would bring a far better income. Galileo traveled back home to Florence from Vallombrosa and, although his dream of joining the order had ended, he continued his education at a school managed by the Camaldolese monks.

Medical Studies Are Discarded in Favor of Physics and Astronomy

When he was 17, Galileo moved back to Pisa to attend the University of Pisa and earn a degree in medicine according to his father's wishes. Galileo was obedient but he never became interested in his medical studies. Instead, he began to focus on the subjects that drew his attention, such as mathematics, natural philosophy, and particularly physics.

Career as a Math Tutor Begins

Each summer, Galileo returned home to Florence during school break, and while his father pushed him to study medicine, he

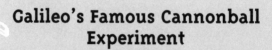

Galileo's Famous Cannonball Experiment

It was during his student years at Pisa that Galileo conducted his legendary experiment with gravity and mass. Up until this time, the theories of Aristotle (384–322 B.C.E.) and Ptolemy (ca. 87–150 C.E.) had remained unquestioned, not just on astronomy but on everything. That included Aristotle's conclusions about falling objects, which Galileo decided to put to the test.

Aristotle wrote that heavier objects fall faster than lighter ones. He further stated that an object weighing twice as much as another would fall twice as fast. This meant that, according to Aristotle, an object weighing 50 pounds would fall 50 times faster than an object weighing one pound.

To test this theory, Galileo climbed to the top of the famous leaning tower in Pisa and dropped two cannonballs of very different weights, or, more precisely, of very different masses. Time and again, they arrived on the ground at the exact same moment, proving that objects of different masses fell at the same rate. This is only one of the experiments that he conducted at Pisa, and it was highly apparent that he had a gift for reasoning in the fields of mathematics and physics.

stubbornly concentrated on mathematics. It was during one of these summers, in 1583, that Galileo attempted to change his father's mind about his interests. He invited one of his university professors, Ostilio Ricci, to come to his home and talk to his father. Ricci tried to convince Galilei that his son's talents lay in the way of math, not medicine. Reluctantly, his father allowed him to study mathematics, such as the writings of the Greek philosophers and mathematicians Archimedes of Syracuse (287–212

B.C.E.) and Euclid of Alexandria (ca. 325–265 B.C.E.), providing that Galileo continue his medical studies at Pisa. Despite this arrangement, in 1585 Galileo quit his medical studies at Pisa without finishing his degree and began teaching mathematics privately in Florence and Siena. Now he was free to explore the discipline he so enjoyed, away from the pressure put upon him by his father to become something he was not.

By 1586, he was back at Vallombrosa, this time as a teacher of math rather than as a student. While at Vallombrosa, he wrote a book called *La balancitta* (The little balance) in which he explained Archimedes' technique of finding the density of objects using a balance scale. The next year Galileo went to visit a professor of mathematics in Rome named Christopher Clavius (1538–1612), who taught at the Collegio Romano, a Jesuit seminary founded by Ignatius Loyola in 1551. Galileo took with him his personal experiments and findings on the subject of the center of gravities. He had heard that the Jesuit mathematicians were fond of the subject and thought that if he could impress them with his work he might be able to obtain an appointment as a professor at the University of Bologna. Clavius was duly impressed, yet Galileo did not win the job.

Galileo left Rome without work, yet he gained a friend in Clavius. By 1588, they were writing each other regularly and exchanging mathematical notes. By now, Galileo had begun to make a reputation for himself through lectures given on mathematics at the Florence Academy and the strong support given him by Christopher Clavius. When, in 1589, the University of Pisa found it was in need of a mathematics professor, Galileo was chosen for the task. This was a fine step forward for Galileo, but he looked ahead to larger career goals.

During the time he spent teaching at Pisa, Galileo wrote a series of unpublished essays titled *De motu* (On motion), in which he describes the theory of motion. He did not view the series as a complete work, which is perhaps why he never had it published. Many of the ideas it held were not correct, but it did address the important issue that through experiments one could come to relative conclusions. The Greeks were responsible for cementing the practice of arriving at conclusions purely through debate. That is to say, by talking something through to its end, people could arrive at answers. Galileo, on the other hand, was a believer in experiments and observations, not speculation. In *De motu*, for example, he discusses how using a sloping plane to slow the rate of descent can test the theory of falling masses.

Galileo Adopts Copernicanism

Galileo had been at the University of Pisa for three years when, in 1591, his father died. As he was the eldest, the burden of supporting the family now fell to him. He would have to find a better-paying job. He received strong support from the independently wealthy nobleman Guidobaldo del Monte (1545–1607) and, in 1592, received an appointment as professor of mathematics at the University of Padua, Italy, adequately boosting his income. His duties at Padua were to teach Euclidian geometry and the Ptolemaic Earth-centered system of astronomy. Astronomy was important for students, especially medical students, to be able to keep a calendar and to be able to use astrology in daily medical practices. The Ptolemaic system annoyed Galileo, as it had Copernicus. By this time, Galileo had studied and accepted Copernicus's theories of a Sun-centered model of the solar system, yet aside from a personal letter he sent in 1598 to a friend, the German astronomer Johannes Kepler, declaring his support of Copernicanism, he kept his views to himself. To go against the accepted system of astronomy was to go against the doctrine of the Catholic Church. He did not want to be branded as a heretic. Then, too, there was the public in general. Although it was the Renaissance, during which freethinking and new ideas were gaining popularity, people as a whole remained overly superstitious and were not receptive to radical change.

Galileo was content at Padua and remained there for 17 very productive years, carrying out new studies and experiments in mechanics, a branch of physics. For example, in 1597, he developed a geometric compass, also called a sector, for use as a computing device, which was mass-marketed along with a manual on how to use it. Compasses are still used for geometrical drawing today. He also developed the thermoscope, a thermometer to measure air temperature. It was in 1599 in Padua that he met and fell in love with a woman named Maria Gamba, from Venice, who would soon become his mistress.

The New Star and the Telescope

In 1604, an event happened that would cause Galileo to take the risk and publicly argue that Copernicus's heliocentric theory was right and Ptolemy's geocentric theory was wrong. A new star appeared in the constellation Serpentarius, one that would come to be known as "Kepler's supernova," even though several persons had witnessed it, including Clavius in Rome. Using parallax observa-

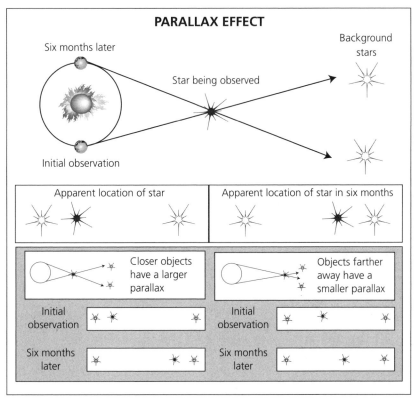

A parallax is the apparent motion of an object against a background due to the motion of the viewer. The object is located closer than the background. In astronomy, stars observed as having a larger parallax were known to be closer to Earth than stars that had a lesser parallax. This method of observation provides a limited but initial piece of information about the distance to stars.

tions, Galileo confirmed that the "new star" must exist very far away and could not possibly exist within the sublunary region (the boundary between the Earth and Moon) of Earth, as was the common belief at the time. No one believed his conclusions, and, wisely, he chose not to push the issue.

A few years later he learned something amazing that would assist him in proving that the Earth truly was in motion around the Sun. In May 1609, Galileo received a letter from a friend who reported that while in Venice he saw a Dutchman named Jan Lippershey showing off his invention of a monocular, or a spyglass, made of lenses that could cause objects at great distances to appear closer. Shortly after making many celestial discoveries with this new instrument, Galileo wrote *Sidereus nuncius* (The starry messenger). A quotation from Galileo in *Sidereus nuncius*, as translated by author and historian Stillman Drake in his book *Discoveries and Opinions of Galileo*, states:

> About ten months ago a report reached my ears that a certain Fleming had constructed a spyglass by means of which visible objects, though very distant from the eye of the observer, were distinctly seen as if nearby. Of this truly remarkable effect several experiences were related, to which some persons gave credence while others denied them. A few days later the report was confirmed to me in a letter from a noble Frenchman at Paris, Jacques Badovere, which caused me to apply myself wholeheartedly to inquire into the means by which I might arrive at the invention of a similar instrument. This I did shortly afterwards, my basis being the theory of refraction.

By using nothing more than his friend's written description of these lenses, Galileo was able to construct practically overnight a *refracting* telescope, and owing to his skills and knowledge of mathematics, it was at once greatly improved over Lippershey's version.

Using materials at hand, Galileo's first telescope had a *magnification* factor of only four, but after he experimented with grinding his own lenses, he finally produced a telescope with a magnification factor of about nine. He eventually took his creation to the Venetian Senate, which bought from him the rights to manufacture it. Within two months after producing his telescope, Galileo had made more startling new discoveries than any astronomer before

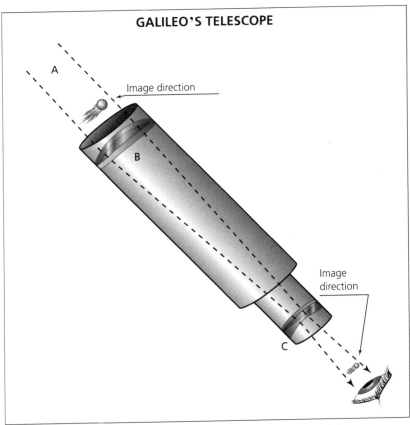

GALILEO'S TELESCOPE

A

Image direction

B

Image
direction

C

Galileo's telescope worked by allowing light to enter at the skyward end (a) then pass though a plano convex—an outward-bulging lens (b)—which bent the light rays. He then placed a plano concave lens (c) ahead of the focal point—the point where the light rays would cross—producing the magnified virtual image. Galileo's best telescope magnified at 32 power (32X). Average modern pair binoculars magnify between 10X and 20X.

him. In *Sidereus nuncius*, he recorded discoveries such as that the Milky Way was made of tiny distant stars, that there were mountains on the Moon, and that rings existed around Saturn. He also discovered the occurrence of sunspots, on which he reported in his *Discourse on Floating Bodies* (1612) and *Letters on the Sunspots* (1613).

On January 7, 1610, he discovered three bright stars near Jupiter and then, six days later, a fourth. These he determined to be Jupiter's moons, orbiting the planet in obvious regularity. This was very important toward proving the theory of a heliocentric solar

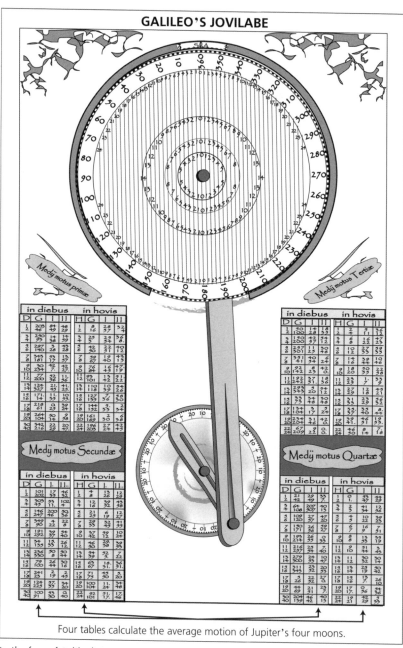

Four tables calculate the average motion of Jupiter's four moons.

In the face of Galileo's instrument, two rotating discs of differing diameters are connected in such a way as to be used in determining the position of the Sun and the Earth's Moon in relationship to the positions of Jupiter's moons.

system. He named the moons of Jupiter the Medicean stars and sent the grand duke of Tuscany, Cosimo de Medici II, a telescope of his own. He did this in the hopes of impressing the duke enough to obtain a new job. His efforts worked, and in 1610, one month after publishing *Sidereus nuncius*, he took a position at the University of Pisa as head mathematician. His only duties were to act as the grand duke's personal mathematician and philosopher.

It was around this time that Galileo invented the Jovilabe, a device used to predict the positions of Jupiter's moons. He developed this instrument in an attempt to solve the problem of determining longitude at sea by using the clockwork movements of Jupiter's moons, for in order to calculate longitude, one needed an accurate means of keeping time. (The English inventor John Harrison developed the first accurate marine chronometer in 1735.) It became impossible, however, for Galileo to produce a Jovilabe that would work well from the rocking deck of a ship; therefore, his instrument could be used only on land and was useless as a navigational aid for seafarers. Still, it was a remarkable piece of work and a fine example of his skill as a mathematician and astronomer.

Copernicanism Deserves Support

For the time being, Galileo was a celebrity. Word of his observations and discoveries spread throughout Rome. In 1611, he was invited to attend a grand banquet at the Collegio Romano, where Jesuit mathematicians certified his discoveries. While there, he gained a membership to the Accademia dei Lincei (Lincei National Academy) by Federigo Cesi, an Italian natural scientist who suggested the word *telescope* for Galileo's invention. Cesi remained a supporter of Galileo for the rest of his life.

By 1612, Galileo had made enough observations of Jupiter's moons to establish accurate periods, but since he had forgotten to consider the motion of the Earth around the Sun, his conclusions were inconsistent. He had also made extensive observations of Saturn, which at first appeared to him as three bodies, a large one in the center with two smaller ones on each side (the smaller bodies being, in reality, the rings). He also determined that Venus had *phases*, as the Moon did, and concluded that the planet must orbit the Sun and not the Earth. All these discoveries pointed to a rotating Earth that in turn revolved around the Sun. He argued his conclusions publicly, claiming that this was proof enough to condemn the Ptolemaic system in favor of the Copernican. His opponents, however, argued that if the Earth were spinning, everything would fly off. They argued further that if the Earth truly were spinning, cannonballs dropped from a high tower could not fall straight down. As the Earth rotated, they would drop behind the tower while they fell. Galileo knew differently, but he could not convince them that the Earth was in motion.

Then, in 1614, a well-known preacher named Tommaso Caccini labeled Galileo a heretic, along with any other mathematician who dared to support the Copernican system. His sermon started rumors of a scandal. By the next year, Caccini was confident enough to offer an official declaration to the Roman Inquisition, which was an organization within the Catholic Church that was in

Consequences of Nonconformity

Giordano Bruno (1548–1600) was an Italian astronomer who also embraced the Copernican theory of a heliocentric solar system. He openly disagreed with the Catholic Church's accepted Ptolemaic theory of a geocentric solar system and sought to teach Copernicanism. The church denounced him, and Bruno fled Italy, fearing punishment for his beliefs. For a few years, he taught abroad, but in 1592 he was located, arrested, and tried by the Roman Inquisition. After years spent in the courts, in 1600, Bruno—who never abandoned his beliefs—was burned at the stake in Rome. Bruno was made an example of the consequences to be suffered if one were to publicly turn from the church.

charge of suppressing known heretics. Galileo wrote a lengthy letter to the influential Monsignor Piero Dini in Rome defending his views, but the cardinals Robert Bellarmine and Paolo Antonio Foscarini warned Piero Dini and Galileo to treat the Copernican theory as merely a suggestion.

The Inquisition

Galileo wrote another letter, this one to the grand duchess Christina of Lorraine, again defending his views but also addressing the relationship between science and scripture. According to Stillman Drake's translation of an excerpt of the letter in his *Discoveries*, Galileo wrote:

> I hold the Sun to be situated motionless in the center of the revolution of the celestial orbs while the Earth rotates on its axis and revolves about the Sun. I support this position not only by refuting the arguments of Ptolemy and Aristotle, but by producing many counter arguments; in particular, some which relate to physical effects whose causes can perhaps be assigned in no other way. There are astronomical arguments derived from many things in my new celestial discoveries that plainly confute the Ptolemaic System while admirably agreeing with and confirming the contrary hypothesis. These men (Galileo's opponents) have resolved to fabricate a shield for their fallacies out of the mantle of pretended religion and the authority of the Bible.

The letter did no good. The Roman Inquisition continued its investigation and while it did not take action against Galileo, in 1616 it officially announced that to support Copernicanism was heretical and went against the teachings of the church and God. Galileo traveled to Rome in order to defend himself in person, figuring he had enough evidence to back a defense and his belief in Copernicanism. In the end, however, Pope Paul V forbade him to hold Copernican views.

In 1618, he lost the confidence of the Jesuits when three bright comets appeared in the sky. Galileo wrote about them in *Discorso delle comete* (Discourse on the comets, 1619), the theory of which was published under the name Mario Guiducci, one of his pupils.

(As a result of the warning given to him from the Roman Inquisition, Galileo published no works under his own name between 1616 and 1623). *Discorso delle comete* was written as a lecture in direct response to an earlier lecture given by the Jesuit mathematician Orazio Grassi of Collegio Romano called *De tribus cometis* (On the three comets), in which Grassi's explanation of the location of the comets attempted to discredit the Copernican theory. Galileo's views published in *Discorso delle comete* attacked this interpretation of these bodies and their location in the heavens. (At the time, Grassi was writing under a surname and Galileo did not know he was attacking the Jesuits until it was too late.) Grassi countered Galileo's *Discorso delle comete* with a work he called *Libra* (The balance). In 1622, Galileo wrote yet another counter to Grassi, entitled *Saggiatore* (The assayer), in which Galileo formulated the new principles of the scientific method. That is to say, it brought about the agreement of theory through experimentation and observation rather than speculation through debate. In 1623, Roman censors granted Galileo the right to publish *Saggiatore*. He dedicated this book to his longtime admirer Maffeo Barberini, recently elected as the new Pope Urban VIII.

By this time, Galileo's health was starting to fail; however, this did not keep him from beginning work on his famous book *Dialogo sopra i due massimi sistemi del mondo, tolemaico copernicano* (Dialogue concerning the two chief systems of the world—Ptolemaic and Copernican), also known simply as *The Dialogue*. Galileo was given permission to write *The Dialogue* providing he presented the Ptolemaic theory in tandem with the Copernican theory, the latter of which he was directed to treat as hypothetical. In this book, he used the two characters to argue against each other. Galileo used his (ultimately false) theory on the relationship between the Moon and the effect it had on the tides as strong argument in support of Copernicanism.

Galileo Is Condemned as a Heretic

In 1632, Galileo published *The Dialogue* without full permission from the Catholic Church in Rome, which so far had approved only the preface and ending. It was not long afterward that Pope Urban

VIII banned it from sale due to its support of Copernicanism. Galileo was called before the Inquisition in Rome, but did not appear at Rome until 1633, after attempting to recover from an illness. The church isolated him in an apartment and interrogated him for 18 days. On April 30, ill and tired of the fight, Galileo confessed that he might have made too strong a case for Copernicanism in *The Dialogue* and offered to counter it in his next book. Threatening him with torture, the Inquisition sentenced Galileo to life under house arrest for breaching the conditions of the 1616 Inquisition concerning the church's official position on the denouncement of the Copernican theory.

In 1634, Galileo, at age 70, traveled home to Arcetri, near Florence, where he remained under house arrest at his villa. It was during this time that he began writing *Discorso intorno a due nuove scienze attinenti alla meccanica e ai movimenti locali* (Discourse concerning two new sciences of mechanics and local motions), also called *Discourses*, a work that he later had smuggled into Holland in order to publish. This book was a great mathematical creation that included his experiments with the pendulum, his developed ideas of the inclined plane and the concepts of speed and acceleration, and calculated centers of gravity.

In 1637, he lost all sight in his right eye from viewing the Sun through his telescope, and by 1638, the year *Discourses* was published in Holland, he was totally blind. When he asked if he could be released to his house in Florence in order to be closer to his physicians, the Inquisition refused. The Inquisition did not want Galileo to have any social contact with anyone. Galileo remained at Arcetri, where he was finally granted the right to attend church on religious holidays, providing he did not associate with anyone. While handicapped by blindness, in 1641 Galileo succeeded in laying out designs for a pendulum clock, as this was a subject that he had long understood but had never taken the time to develop. (His son Vincenzio tried to build the clock from his father's design without success.) On the evening of January 8, 1642, Galileo died in his villa as a condemned man.

On October 31, 1992, 350 years after Galileo's death, Pope John Paul II gave a speech on behalf of the Catholic Church in which he admitted to errors made on the church's part in the case of Galileo, and he officially declared the case closed. While it is now known that Galileo's theories were correct, Pope John Paul II never admitted that the church was mistaken for having convicted Galileo of heresy, since during that era and according to contemporary thinking, the church believed he was indeed a heretic and therefore the conviction was not in error. In his letter to the grand duchess Christina (as translated by Stillman Drake in *Discoveries*) Galileo is quoted as writing: "I do not feel obliged to believe that the same God who has endowed us with sense, reason and intellect has intended us to forgo their use . . ."

CHRONOLOGY

1564	Born February 15 in Pisa, Italy
1574	Moves to Florence and attends school at Camaldolese Monastery at Vallombrosa
1578	Accepted by the Camaldolese order as a novice, but his father insists he withdraw
1581	Begins medical and mathematical studies at Pisa
1585	Gives up his medical studies at Pisa without finishing his degree
1586	Begins teaching mathematics at Vallombrosa and writes a book titled *La Balancitta* (The little balance)
1588	Applies unsuccessfully for the chair in mathematics at Bologna, Italy
1589	Appointed to the chair in mathematics at Pisa
1592	Appointed to the chair in mathematics at the University of Padua, Italy
1597	Invents his geometric and military compass
1604	Observes a new star in the constellation Serpentarius and uses parallax observations to confirm it exists beyond the sublunary sphere

1609	Creates his own nine-powered telescope using the original designs of Dutch lens maker Jan Lippershey
1610	Discovers the moons of Jupiter, publishes *Sidereus nuncius* (The starry messenger), and is appointed mathematician and philosopher to the grand duke of Tuscany, Cosimo de Medici II
1611	Is made a member of the Accademia dei Lincei in honor of his remarkable celestial discoveries
1616	Is warned by Pope Paul V against supporting Copernicanism. The Inquisition officially denounces Copernicanism as heretical.
1623	Publishes his book *Saggiatore* (The assayer), in which he formulates the new principles of the scientific method
1632	Publishes his book *Dialogo sopra i due massimi sistemi del mondo, tolemaico copernicano* (Dialogue concerning two chief world systems, Ptolemaic and Copernican) outlining his support of the Copernican system
1633	Interrogated by the Roman Inquisition, which finds him guilty of showing support for Copernicanism and places him under permanent house arrest
1638	Publishes in Holland his book *Discorso intorno a due nuove scienze attinenti alla meccanica e ai movimenti locali* (Discourse concerning two new sciences of mechanics and local motions)
1642	Dies January 8 in Arcetri, outside Florence, Italy

FURTHER READING

Books

Bendick, Jeanne. *Along Came Galileo.* Sandwich, Mass.: Beautiful Feet Books, 1999. Written in easy-to-follow style, this book about Galileo, his achievements, and his way of life offers the average reader insight into astronomical history.

Boerst, William J. *Galileo Galilei and the Science of Motion (Great Scientists)*. Greensboro, N.C.: Morgan Reynolds, 2002. From Boerst's *Great Scientists* collection, a study on the life of Galileo and his accomplishments in science.

Galilei, Galileo; Stillman Drake, translator. *Discoveries and Opinions of Galileo*. New York: Anchor, 1957. The definitive translations of four of Galileo's writings, *The Starry Messenger, Letter to the Grand Duchess Christina, Letters on Sunspots*, and *The Assayer*.

Goldsmith, Mike. *Galileo Galilei (Scientists Who Made History)*. Austin, Tex.: Raintree/Steck Vaughn, 2002. Offers a well-organized account of Galileo in prose tailored for readers in grades 4–6. Includes illustrations.

MacLachlan, James. *Galileo Galilei: First Physicist (Oxford Portraits in Science)*. New York: Oxford University Press Children's Books, 1999. Tailored for students in grades 6 and up, this book describes Galileo as one of history's foremost scientific minds of his day, giving a clear and concise account of his life.

Taylor, Ina. *Galileo (Beginner's Guide)*. London: Hodder & Stoughton, 2003. A book that introduces the reader to the life, discoveries, and inventions of Galileo in person's terms.

Web Sites

NOVA. "Galileo's Battle for the Heavens" Available online. URL: http://www.pbs.org/wgbh/nova/galileo. Accessed November 29, 2004. Public Broadcasting System (PBS) science Web page offering articles on Galileo.

"Rice University's Galileo Project." Available online. URL: http://es.rice.edu/ES/humsoc/Galileo. Accessed November 29, 2004. A source of information on the life and work of Galileo Galilei and the science of his time.

Johannes Kepler

4

(1571–1630)

Johannes Kepler was the first astronomer to solve the riddle of planetary motion. *(Photo courtesy of AIP Emilio Segrè Visual Archives)*

The Father of Celestial Mechanics

Johannes Kepler was a German astronomer and mathemetician famous for devising what are known today as Kepler's three laws of planetary motion. He demonstrated that the planets, in particular Mars, moved in elliptical orbits, not in circular orbits, as was the belief at the time. He accomplished this by using the accurate, naked-eye observations of Mars recorded by the famous astronomer Tycho Brahe, to whom he was assistant and successor. Kepler advanced the Copernican heliocentric theory of the solar system and demonstrated that planets orbited the Sun in elliptical orbits with the Sun at one focus. By finally solving the riddle of planetary motion, Kepler was a key scientist in modernizing astronomy by extensive use of celestial mechanics.

Born into Poverty

Johannes Kepler was born prematurely on December 27, 1571, in Weil der Stadt, Germany, to Heinrich Kepler, a mercenary soldier, or warrior for hire, and Katherine Kepler, daughter of an innkeeper. Johannes Kepler did not speak well of either of his parents in later life. He was always a weak and sickly child, and much of his life was spent in ill health. He contracted smallpox at a very young age and suffered from poor vision.

In 1576, his parents moved to nearby Leonberg, Germany, then to Ellmendingen, Germany, then back to Leonberg. This unstable lifestyle made it difficult for Johannes to attend elementary school. More often, he was put to work at the inn of his maternal grandfather. Despite his sporadic education, Johannes displayed uncommon intelligence and insatiable curiosity—an important fact to consider, since it was during these early inquisitive years that he was first introduced to astronomy.

When he was six, his mother took him to observe the famous 1577 comet, discovered by Danish astronomer Tycho Brahe (1546–1601). This event made a lasting impression on the young boy, sparking his first interest in the stars. Then, in 1580, at age nine, he was privileged to witness a full lunar eclipse. This was another event that fueled the scientific ember that had begun burning within him. One must remember, though, that during Kepler's time an astronomer was considered more accurately as an astrologer, whose job it was to study the stars simply to cast predictions and manage the calendar.

Scholarship Advancement

It was not until he was 13 that Kepler finally finished his elementary Latin school in Leonberg. In 1584, he entered a Protestant seminary at Adelberg (formerly Hundsholz), Germany. Given his high intelligence, feeble health, and deep devotion to religion, Kepler's goal was to become ordained in the Protestant ministry, which would allow him a quiet life. In 1589, he began his university education at the Protestant University of Tübingen, Germany. Kepler was a poor man and unable to fund his own education; however, the Protestant dukes of Württemberg had devised an advanced public education system that included scholarships for the less advantaged in order to educate more clergymen in the new Protestant faith. This program provided the means for Kepler to attend the university. He concentrated on theology and philosophy, but also studied mathematics and astronomy.

It was not long before Kepler's astronomy professor, Michael Maestlin (1550–1631), one of the leading astronomers of the day, introduced him to the controversial Copernican system. Maestlin openly taught Ptolemaic astronomy, yet secretly believed in the Copernican system. Upon discovering Kepler's keen mind, Maestlin selected him as one of his pupils for the more advanced mathematics. This meant acquainting him with the details of Copernicanism. It did not take long for Kepler to become convinced that the Copernican system was the correct model of the universe, for in his mind the simple harmony of the heliocentric system was far more appealing than the complexity of the Ptolemaic system. He also learned at this time that Copernicus did not write the foreword to *De revolutionibus orbium coelestium* (On the revolutions of the celestial orbits) that stated the book was only an abstract mathematical hypothesis; in fact, it was written by the overseeing publisher, Andrew Osiander.

A Surprise Career in Mathematics and Astronomy

In 1591, Kepler passed his exams and received a master's degree in arts. For three more years, he stayed on at Tübingen, attending graduate courses in theology, still aiming toward a life in the Protestant ministry. Even though he was a genius at mathematics and even more enthusiastic (and far more outspoken) about Copernicanism than was Professor Maestlin, he had never considered a career other than ecclesiastical. Therefore, it was a surprise when, in 1594, he was offered a professorship in mathematics and astronomy at the Protestant University of Gratz, Styria (now part of Austria). This offer came about after an inquiry from the Gratz governors to the Tübingen Senate, asking for a recommendation for a mathematics teacher to replace theirs, who had recently died. The Tübingen Senate recommended Kepler for two reasons: first, he was a skilled mathematician, and second, he was an open advocate for Copernicanism, which was not associated with true men of God. Considering his heretical devotion to Copernicanism, the Senate secretly decided it was best that Kepler be steered away from a career in the church.

After a short time of indecision, Kepler finally accepted the job, and in April 1594, he arrived in Gratz. Part of his duties as mathematician and astronomer was to cast astrological predictions. Kepler deeply believed in a kindred link between humankind and the cosmos; however, he also believed that basing astrological predictions on a faulty (Ptolemaic) system was foolhardy. Despite his distaste for the conventional methods, Kepler predicted a cold winter ahead and a Turkish invasion, both of which came true. This earned him new respect and an increase in salary.

A Restless Mind

It turned out that Kepler was not a good teacher, and his classes were very small. This provided plenty of time for his preoccupation with studying the Copernican system. Eventually, he began to ask himself questions regarding Copernicus's heliocentric system. Copernicus still relied on much of the ancient data, such as having to employ epicycles to the planets' perfectly circular orbits in order to explain their retrograde motion. Kepler asked: Why did the planets describe perfect circles around the Sun? Why were there only six planets in the solar system, and why were they so evenly spaced? Kepler studied Copernicus's *De revolutionibus orbium coelestium*, sorting through the problems, and always, in the back of his mind, the mysterious construct of the solar system called for his attention.

One day during a class lecture, Kepler divined a first theory to augment the heliocentric model. As he was drawing for his class a

The Five Regular Solids

In geometry, the five regular solids are three-dimensional geometric objects with equal sides. For a shape to qualify as a regular solid it must satisfy two conditions: first, the faces of a polyhedron are polygons of the same type, and second, the same number of polygons converge at each of the vertexes.

Only these five shapes can be used to make perfectly symmetrical three-dimensional forms with equal faces. Each solid can be inscribed inside a sphere where all corners, or vertices, touch the wall of the sphere. In the same way, each solid can be circumscribed outside a sphere with its surface touching on the exact center of each face of the solid.

In Kepler's book *Mysterium cosmographicum* (Secrets of the universe, 1596), his nesting model and use of the five solids turned out to be wrong. The placement of the planets in the solar system are not symmetrical

THE FIVE REGULAR SOLIDS

Vertice

Edge

Face

Tetrahedron

4 vertices
6 edges
4 faces

Cube

8 vertices
12 edges
6 faces

Octahedron

6 vertices
12 edges
8 faces

Dodecahedron

20 vertices
30 edges
12 faces

Icosahedron

12 vertices
30 edges
20 faces

Kepler devised a model of the solar system based on the uniformity of the regular polyhedra, also called the regular solids. Only these five shapes can be used to make perfectly symmetrical three-dimensional forms with equal faces.

in nature but are determined by the gravitational influence on their mass from the Sun and the other planets.

geometric figure of a triangle fit between two circles, it suddenly occurred to him that the figure looked very much like the Copernican orbits of Saturn and Jupiter.

Then he had a sudden inspiration. To him, it was clear that the ratios between the orbits of Saturn and Jupiter and the ratios between the two concentric circles and the triangle were the same. He attempted to further inscribe a two-dimensional square between Jupiter and Mars, a pentagon between Mars and Earth, and a hexagon between Earth and Venus, and, lastly, an octagon between Venus and Mars. He could not make this "even spacing of the planets" hypothesis work, yet he felt he had stumbled onto something important. His restless mind continued to dwell on the math. Then he hit on a new theory! What about a three-dimensional universe? Perhaps he should be thinking in terms of spheres, not in circles. He devised a model built on nesting spheres and regular polyhedra, also called the regular solids, or Platonic solids.

Kepler Attempts to Lend Proof to Copernicanism

Kepler was very enthusiastic when he connected the fact that there were five regular polyhedra and likewise five spaces between the six planets of the solar system. The mystic in him was convinced that there was no way this could be a coincidence. The religious man in him believed that God must have created the universe from a perfect mathematical plan, and since humans were made in the image of God, they were likewise capable of deducing its secrets. Finally, Kepler had an answer to his question as to why there were just six planets. In his mind, the construct of the universe must exist in symmetry and perfect harmony. That is to say, by using the perfection of the five solids as a framework, he could explain the symmetrical placement of the planets, of which, during that time, only six were known to exist.

In Kepler's model, the outer sphere represented Saturn, where one would envision the planet in orbit along the equator. The nesting sequence went as such: a cube between Saturn and the sphere representing Jupiter; a tetrahedron between Jupiter and the sphere representing Mars; a dodecahedron between Mars and the sphere representing Earth; an icosahedron between Earth and the sphere representing Venus; and an octahedron between the sphere representing Venus and the sphere representing Mercury. Kepler had devised a geometric key to unlocking the secrets of the solar system. He was so convinced he had solved the problem that he blamed the discrepancies in some of the distances on errors in Copernicus's tables. Unfortunately, this theory proved to be wrong.

One question had been solved (in Kepler's mind), but there was another, a question no astronomer before him had ever raised. Why did the outer planets orbit more slowly than the inner ones? For example, the first planet, Mercury, takes just three months to orbit the Sun, and in contrast, the sixth and last planet, Saturn,

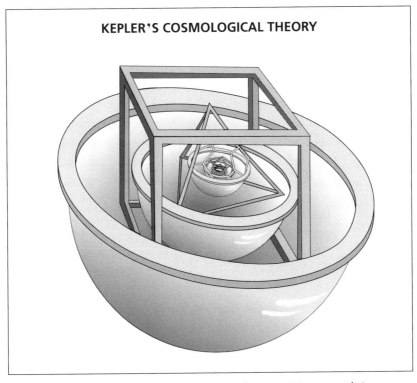

KEPLER'S COSMOLOGICAL THEORY

In Kepler's 1597 work *Mysterium cosmographicum* (Secrets of the universe), he argued in favor of Copernicanism, stating that the five regular solids determined the distances of the planets from the central Sun, and one another, meaning a planet's orbit was circumscribed around one solid and inscribed within another.

takes 30 years. Kepler decided that an invisible force emanating from the Sun that grew weaker as it traveled away, much the same as light, drove the planets.

He put forth his conclusions in a book titled *Mysterium cosmographicum* (Secrets of the universe), which he published in 1596. Kepler saw his theory as providing evidence in support of Copernicanism. He sent a copy of his book to all the leading scholars, including Tycho Brahe, the famous Danish astronomer. Brahe, he learned, was impressed with his work. Though he did not agree with the heliocentric model, Brahe recognized Kepler's genius and asked him repeatedly to visit Uraniborg. Kepler declined, stating an unwillingness to travel such a great distance. Also, he was in the middle of negotiating an arranged marriage pressed upon him by friends. In 1597, he married a widow named Barbara Muehleck.

He Assists a Master

In 1598, Archduke Ferdinand of Hapsburg, a Catholic, closed down the university where Kepler taught, along with other Protestant schools, in an attempt to abolish the Protestant religion. The archduke allowed Kepler to stay on for a while; however, the following year he had to choose between converting to the Catholic faith or leaving. Kepler was not inclined to change his faith, yet he had nowhere to go. Tübingen would not take him due to his heretical Copernican views. Thus, he credited divine intervention when, in 1600, he learned that the great astronomer Tycho Brahe was now living in Prague as the chief astronomer to Emperor Rudolph II and was looking for an assistant. Kepler took the job at once, and on January 1, 1600, he and his family departed Gratz to join Brahe in Prague.

Kepler was excited about working for Brahe. His mass of observational data was well known, and Kepler believed he could use his data to study the orbits of the planets in support of Copernicanism. Brahe had other goals. He was interested only in furthering his own model, not that of Copernicus's, with whom he disagreed. Brahe was selfish with his data and set Kepler to work studying only the data on the eccentricities of Mars's orbit, which was considered to be the most difficult of all the planets. This was fortunate for Kepler and the advancement of astronomy in general, for it was the study of Mars, the planet with the most elliptical (oval) orbit in the solar system, that ultimately led to him to formulate the correct laws of planetary motion.

The New Master Battles with Mars

After Kepler had worked with Brahe for only 18 months, the Danish astronomer died in 1601 from what is believed today to have been mercury poisoning. Kepler soon succeeded Brahe as imperial astronomer for Emperor Rudolph II. Working quickly, Kepler seized all of Brahe's astronomical logs. Later, when the Brahe family was settling Tycho's estate, Kepler was grudgingly allowed to keep this written data; however, he was denied the use of Brahe's observational instruments, which later became lost.

In possession now of all Brahe's logs, Kepler continued to labor over the thus far inexplicable orbit of Mars. For eight years, he worked on the problem, despite having once proclaimed that he would have the riddle solved in eight days. In the beginning, he insisted on applying the customary perfect circles to its orbit. He met with no success, and time marched steadily onward as Kepler encountered one defeat after another.

In a final act of frustration, he discarded all his previous learning on the dynamics of orbits and began to formulate a new science. In other words, Kepler did away with traditional thinking, which kept planets in perfect orbits and, for the first time, applied physics to astronomy. He first reexamined the motion of Earth, coming to the conclusion that the speed of its orbit was not uniform, as was then believed, but instead fluctuated. He determined that as the planet neared the Sun, the speed of its orbit increased and likewise, as it moved farther from the Sun, its orbital speed decreased. He then stated that there was a force present in the Sun that directly affected the motion of the planets. As a result of Kepler's work, he determined that the planets did not move in perfect circles. They moved in ellipses, or slight ovals. The orbital eccentricities were not great, but were enough do away with the belief in circular orbits and fully explain planetary retrograde motion while keeping the Sun in the fixed center of the solar system. Kepler had finally solved the mystery behind true planetary motion.

The Formulation of Kepler's Laws

In Prague, Kepler spent 10 fruitful years in the service of Emperor Rudolph II. While he busied himself working out the mechanics of the solar system based on Brahe's observations of Mars, he was also breaking new ground in other areas of science.

In 1604, he published *Astronomia pars optica* (The optical part of astronomy), concerning the study of optics. In this book, Kepler addressed many firsts. For example, he was the first to correctly explain the function of the human eye, with the upside-down picture that appears on the back of the retina and how both eyes are used in depth perception. He was first to address atmospheric refraction and the first to hypothesize on the use of optic glass to improve nearsightedness or farsightedness.

By 1606, he finished and published his book *De stella nova* (Concerning the new star) on the supernova of 1604, commonly called Kepler's supernova. Then, in 1609, he published his most notorious work, *Astronomia nova* (New astronomy), outlining his first two laws of planetary motion.

In 1610, Kepler heard about a new observational instrument called a telescope, devised by Italian astronomer Galileo Galilei (1564–1642). He wrote a letter of support that he published under the title *Dissertatio cum nuncio sidereo* (Conversation with the sidereal messenger). Later that year, he acquired his own telescope and made observations of Jupiter and its moons. He recorded his findings and, in another gesture of support toward Galileo, published them in a book titled *Narratio de observatis quatuor jovis satellitibus* (Narration about four satellites of Jupiter observed).

The following year, Kepler spent time experimenting with the telescope and lenses. He then published *Dioptrice* (Dioptrics), in which he addressed the first study of the properties of lenses. In

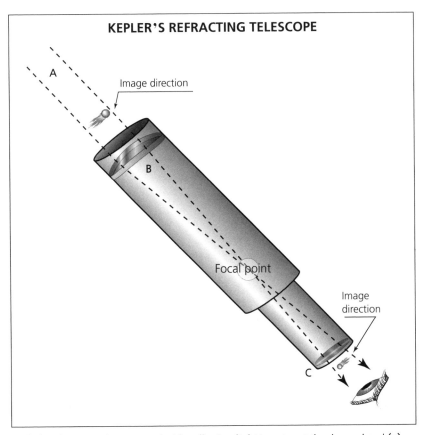

KEPLER'S REFRACTING TELESCOPE

A

Image direction

B

Focal point

Image direction

C

Kepler's refracting telescope worked by allowing light to enter at the skyward end (a) then pass through a plano convex—outward bulging lens (b)—which bent the light rays. The point at which they cross is called the focal point. The light then passes through the convex lens of the eyepiece (c), magnifying the image for the viewer.

Dioptrice, he presented a new telescope design that would eventually be called a refracting telescope, which uses two convex lenses that invert and magnify an image.

In the same year that *Dioptrice* was published, Kepler lost his wife, Barbara, and six-year-old son Friedrich to illness. Then Emperor Rudolph II abdicated his throne to his brother, Matthias, a devout Catholic who, unlike Rudolph, did not lend support to Protestants. This marked the beginning of the end for Kepler's long list of scientific achievements. They had reached their peak and were about to start a gradual descent.

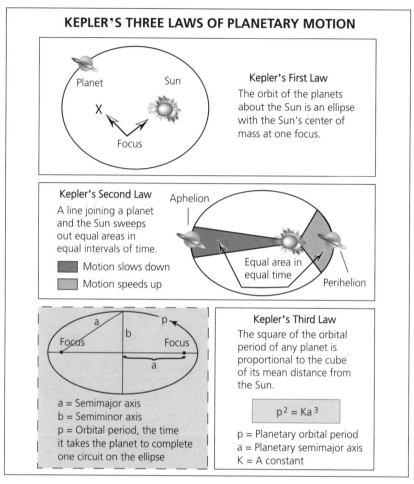

KEPLER'S THREE LAWS OF PLANETARY MOTION

Kepler's First Law
The orbit of the planets about the Sun is an ellipse with the Sun's center of mass at one focus.

Kepler's Second Law
A line joining a planet and the Sun sweeps out equal areas in equal intervals of time.

Motion slows down
Motion speeds up

Equal area in equal time

Aphelion
Perihelion

a = Semimajor axis
b = Semiminor axis
p = Orbital period, the time it takes the planet to complete one circuit on the ellipse

Kepler's Third Law
The square of the orbital period of any planet is proportional to the cube of its mean distance from the Sun.

$$p^2 = Ka^3$$

p = Planetary orbital period
a = Planetary semimajor axis
K = A constant

Kepler published his first two laws of planetary motion in his 1609 work, *Astronima nova*. His third law appeared in his 1619 work, *Harmonice mundi*. The elliptical orbits shown here are exaggerated. A planet's true orbit is only slightly elliptic.

As a Protestant in a Catholic empire suddenly under the rule of a new king, Kepler was forced to leave Prague. In 1612 he gathered up the remainder of his family and moved to Linz, Austria, where he took a job as provincial mathematician. By 1613, he met and married Susanna Reuttinger, the daughter of a cabinetmaker.

In Linz, Kepler's duties required him to produce astronomical tables based on Brahe's astronomical logs. He also went to work refining his laws of planetary motion. By 1619, he had worked out his third law (which laid the groundwork for the English physist

Sir Isaac Newton (1642–1727) to derive the law of universal gravitation). In 1619, he published the third law in *Harmonice mundi* (Harmony of the world). Kepler's pioneering efforts on celestial motion were finally finished, and his work in *Harmonice mundi* and *Astronomia nova* together came to be known as Kepler's three laws of planetary motion:

- The orbit of any planet is an ellipse with the Sun at one focus.
- The line joining a planet and the Sun sweeps out equal areas in equal intervals of time.
- The ratio of the squares of the periods of any two planets is equal to the ratio of the cubes of their mean distances from the Sun.

During the same year that *Harmonice mundi* was published, Emperor Matthias died, which brought about the eventual placement of Emperor Ferdinand II to the throne, heralding the onset of the Thirty Years' War. This was the same Archduke Ferdinand of Hapsburg who was responsible for closing down the Protestant school where Kepler taught. The Thirty Years' War was a conflict between Protestants and Catholics that began in 1618 and ended in 1648.

Kepler's War against Witchery

Beginning in 1615, as Kepler worked on his *Harmonice mundi*, officials denounced his mother, Katherine, as a witch. Kepler came to her defense, and after a lengthy trial lasting six years, during which time his 72-year-old mother spent 14 months incarcerated in chains, the charges were finally dropped. His mother died six months after her acquittal.

Even as he waged an expensive legal battle on behalf of his mother, Kepler managed to forge ahead with his scientific work. In 1617, he published his largest work, *Epitome astronomiae copernicanae* (Epitome of Copernican astronomy), in which he applied his newly formulated celestial mechanics not only to Mars but to all the planets, including Earth's moon. This book was a revision of Copernicus's theories and, in truth, should be considered as the new Keplerian system. *Epitome astronomiae copernicanae* was momentous in the furthering of modern astronomy in the fact that Kepler's universal model had completely, and correctly, done away with perfect circles and epicycles, which were still present in other astronomical publications of the scientific revolution, even those of Galileo.

The Crowning Achievement

As the years passed in Linz, Kepler continued to produce a varied array of pamphlets, books, ephemerides, and calendars. There was one unfinished publication, however, that everyone from navigators to calendar makers had been waiting to see: the completion of the *Tabulae rudolphinae* (Rudolphine tables), which were the contemporary star tables based on Tycho Brahe's lifework, begun by Brahe before his death and named for Emperor Rudolph II. For 22 years, Kepler had harbored the information, working on it here and there, but never completing it. Finally, in 1627, after struggling with money and delays caused by war, the long-awaited *Tabulae rudolphinae* saw publication. The work consisted of tables and rules for predicting the future positions of the planets. It cataloged 1,005 stars, expanded by Kepler from Brahe's original 777 stars. The *Tabulae rudolphinae* predictions were doubly more accurate than previous methods and remained valuable for more than a century.

The printing of the *Tabulae rudolphinae* was not an easy task. The publication procedures were left entirely up to Kepler, and the duty taxed his strength. Linz had no printing press for such a large work, leaving Kepler to travel the countryside in search of funds and a suitable press. Boils and piles (hemorrhoids) forced him to alternate between riding on horseback and walking on foot the miles upon miles he had to travel. Despite the obstacles, he finally located an appropriate printer in Ulm, Germany. Having never liked Linz, Kepler happily moved his family to Ulm and saw the manuscript through. During the four-year-long process of getting the *Tabulae rudolphinae* to press, however, the constant strain on his already feeble body began to permanently weaken him. Due to his body's frail state, Kepler was beginning to lose heart in his work.

Kepler himself designed the frontispiece of the *Rudolphine Tables*, which shows a Greek temple with five astronomers: Hipparchus, Ptolemy, Copernicus, Tycho Brahe, and an ancient Babylonian engaged in astronomical debate. On one of the faces in the base, Kepler sits at work behind a table. *(Photo courtesy of NOAA)*

In 1628, Albrecht von Wallenstein, generalissimo to Emperor Ferdinand II and duchy of Friedland and Sagan, Germany, offered Kepler a position as his astrologer. Kepler moved his family to Sagan in order to carry out his duties to Wallenstein, which involved casting horoscopes. Neither man was satisfied with the other. Kepler hated the work, and Wallenstein appeared to want Kepler around merely as a showpiece in court and did not take Kepler seriously. Leaving his family behind, Kepler soon set out from Sagan in search of a new job and to attempt to collect wages still owed to him by the emperor.

On November 2, 1630, Kepler arrived in Ratisbon, Germany, and suddenly fell ill with fever. For days, he grew steadily worse, mumbling incoherently and falling in and out of consciousness. Then, on November 15, 1630, Kepler died with a Protestant minister at his bedside. Four days later, he was buried outside of town in the cemetery of St. Peter, which was later destroyed in the Thirty Years' War.

Kepler's Legacy

Johannes Kepler was a brilliant scientist, sensitive, caring, and humble. In the infancy of modern astronomy and throughout the beginning of the age of reason, he gave his all to humanity without boast or regret, and often he held the work of others in greater appreciation than his own. His lifework helped lay to rest the mystery behind planetary motion and set humankind on the correct path toward understanding the dynamics of the universe. For this sacrifice through the best and worst years of his life, astronomy is truly grateful. Nothing remains of Kepler's tomb. However, his manuscripts survived and were purchased nearly a century later by Catherine II of Russia.

They are now preserved at the Russian Academy of Sciences' Pulkovo Observatory, near St. Petersburg.

CHRONOLOGY

1571	Born on December 27 in Weil der Stadt, Germany
1577	Observes his first comet
1580	Observes his first lunar eclipse
1589	Enters the Protestant University of Tübingen, Germany, where he is introduced to Copernicanism
1591	Receives his master's degree in arts, continues to study theology
1594	Accepts the seat as professor of mathematics at Gratz, Austria
1596	Publishes his famous work *Mysterium cosmographicum* (Secrets of the universe), in which he describes his new model of the universe
1600	Accepts a job in Prague as assistant to Danish astronomer Tycho Brahe
1601	Appointed as Brahe's successor after Brahe's death

1604	Publishes *Astronomia pars optica* (The optical part of astronomy), in which he addresses atmospheric refraction for the first time
1606	Publishes *De stella nova* (Concerning the new star) on the supernova of 1604
1609	Publishes *Astronomia nova* (New astronomy), outlining his first two laws of planetary motion
1610	Publishes *Narratio de observatis quatuor jovis satellitibus* (Narration about four satellites of Jupiter observed) in support of Galileo's discoveries using the newly invented telescope
1611	Publishes *Dioptrice* (Dioptrics), in which he describes his new telescope structure
1612	Forced out of Prague and accepts a job in Linz, Austria
1617	Publishes *Epitome astronomiae copernicanae* (Epitome of Copernican astronomy), a book on heliocentric theory
1619	Publishes *Harmonice mundi* (Harmony of the world), in which he describes his third law of planetary motion
1627	Publishes the *Tabulae rudolphinae* (Rudolphine tables), which contains accurate predictions of the planets' future positions
1630	Dies from illness on November 15 in Ratisbon, Germany

FURTHER READING

Books

Caspar, Max. *Kepler.* New York: Dover Publications, 1993. A definitive biography of Johannes Kepler, translated from German. Introduction and notes by Owen Gingerich.

Kepler, Johannes; A. M. Duncan, translator. *Secrets of the Universe (Mysterium cosmographicum).* New York: Abaris Books, 1981. This is the first English translation of Kepler's original 1596 volume.

Koestler, Arthur. *The Watershed: A Biography of Johannes Kepler.* New York: Doubleday, 1960. A well-written piece outlining the life and scientific accomplishments of Johannes Kepler.

Rosen, Sidney. *The Harmonious World of Johannes Kepler.* Boston: Little, Brown, 1962. A compelling biography of Johannes Kepler written for a younger audience.

Voelkel, James R. *Johannes Kepler and the New Astronomy.* New York: Oxford University Press, 2001. Designed for students in middle school and up, this is an easy-to-follow biography of Johannes Kepler that deals with his discoveries as well as his personal life.

Web Sites

Drennon, William L. "Kepler's Laws." Available online. URL: http://home.cvc.org/science/kepler.htm. Accessed November 29, 2004. An animated Web page outlining Kepler's three laws of planetary motion. Provides a brief history of astronomy and biographies on Kepler and Danish astronomer Tycho Brahe.

Fowler, Michael. "Johannes Kepler." Available online. URL: http://www.phys.virginia.edu/classes/109N/1995/lectures/kepler.html. Accessed November 29, 2004. A brief biography on Johannes Kepler including line drawings, links to other astronomy-oriented lectures, and references.

5

Benjamin Banneker

(1731–1806)

Benjamin Banneker, a free black man in 18th-century America, taught himself astronomy. *(Photo by MPI/News and Sport Collection/ Getty Images)*

The First African-American Astronomer

Eighteenth-century astronomer, clockmaker, farmer, and antislavery advocate, Benjamin Banneker is known as the first African-American astronomer. Banneker did not begin his career in astronomy until he was 57, an age when many people today begin thinking of their retirement. His achievements are even more remarkable given the fact that he lived during the time of slavery in America, when virtually any important accomplishment by an African American, enslaved or free, was suppressed or unnoticed, or the credit was given to the master. Benjamin Banneker proved, through his work in astronomy, his mechanical innovations, and his involvement in the 1791 survey of Washington, D.C., that African Americans deserved as much intellectual credit as anyone else when allowed equal rights and the same chance to succeed as any other person.

Born into Freedom

A descendant of slaves, Benjamin Banneker was born on November 9, 1731, in Ellicott Mills, a small town outside Baltimore, Maryland. Molly Welsh, his grandmother, immigrated to the United States from England. She married a freed slave, Benjamin's grandfather, whose African name was Bannaka. Since she and Bannaka were both free, by law any children born to them would be free as well. The couple's eldest child, Mary, was Benjamin's mother, who married Robert, a former slave originally from Africa.

Benjamin grew up on the family farm and was taught to read from the Bible by his grandmother. At an early age, he displayed uncommon intelligence, caught onto ideas quickly, had a remarkable memory, and soon surpassed even his grandmother in his knowledge of the Scriptures. Having developed beyond what she could teach him, Molly made arrangements for Benjamin to attend a local school for boys, recently established by a Quaker schoolteacher. It was the schoolteacher who was responsible for changing Benjamin's surname from Bannaka to Banneker.

Unlike the other children, during his free time Benjamin was not interested in playing. Instead, he was obsessed by books and the fascinating things he learned every time he opened one. Even as a very young man, it was evident that Benjamin's quest in life was for knowledge.

The Necessities of Farm Life Induce Self-Education

When he was old enough to help till the soil, his brief education at the small school halted. Between the plowing, sowing, reaping, and irrigation of the tobacco crops on his family's farm, little time was left for academics. He nevertheless continued his education on his own, as he would for the rest of his life. He began to advance in mathematics as he worked out formulas in books he had to borrow from the schoolteacher, whose schoolhouse lay miles from the family's isolated farm. The remoteness of the Bannaka farm and beauty of the surroundings imparted to him a special appreciation for nature. Little did he realize that his fascination for natural sciences, coupled with his keen intellect, would someday lead him to discover and then contribute to the science of astronomy.

His First Brush with Notoriety

Banneker's capacity for mathematics was not his only attribute. He also had an exceptional understanding of mechanics, a helpful skill in a region where craftsmen such as tinkers and blacksmiths were in high demand, yet few in number. The success of the family farm was greatly owed to the skill Banneker imparted to irrigation techniques.

In 1751, when Banneker was 21 years old, he saw his first pocket watch. He was fascinated by its intricate construction. Managing to borrow one, he took it home to study and then returned it to the owner. One year later, using only crude tools, his sharp mind, and his photographic memory, he constructed his own timepiece—a wall clock—made primarily of meticulously carved hardwood. (For more than 40 years, it struck on the hour with remarkable precision.) Word of his accomplishment spread, and the public looked upon it as something extraordinary, for personal timepieces during this era were practically nonexistent except among the very wealthy. Sundials and hourglasses were the common timekeepers of the day. In the following years, due to the creation of his clock and his way with mathematics, Benjamin Banneker would come to be respected around the region as a man of learning.

On July 10, 1759, Benjamin's father, Robert Bannaka, died. Sometime within the next few years, his grandmother Molly died. The family farm then fell to the care of Benjamin and his mother, Mary. He isolated himself at the farm, caring for the crops, beehives, and his mother, making few, if any, friends. Now and then an occasional visitor would arrive in need of assistance with mathematical problems or just to see his legendary clock. Otherwise, Banneker, a

Molly Welsh

Benjamin Banneker's grandmother was a British milkmaid from Wessex County, England. The exact spelling of her last name is elusive. Both Welsh and Walsh have been used; however, the more likely of the two is Welsh.

One morning in England, as 17-year-old Molly was doing the milking, the pail overturned, spilling all the milk. Her employer accused her of stealing the milk, and she was quickly arrested. Stealing was an offense that sent the convicted to the gallows. There was a provision in the law, however, that allowed the prisoner to "call for the book." If the felon could read from the Bible, then he or she would be given mercy under the discretion of the king. Molly called for the book and read clearly from the passages. Her life was spared. She was pardoned under the condition that she be exiled from the country for seven years. Commonly, this meant banishment to the American colonies.

For payment of her ocean passage, Molly was to serve seven years labor as a servant in the Americas. This type of payment for passage was called indentured servitude, the length of which was determined before departure. The merchant seamen would then sell the prisoners to awaiting plantation owners across the ocean in the New World. The profits from the sales would then make their way back to England by way of fees.

modest man, kept to himself throughout the years, until one day when industry came to the territory.

An Influential Arrival

In 1772, a family of four brothers by the last name of Ellicott moved into the area. They bought land that flanked the nearby Patapsco River and began a grain mill and a general store. Banneker, now 41 years old, was drawn to the workings of the mill, which employed an

The sea voyage was miserable, cramped, and dirty. With great relief, Molly landed at Chesapeake Bay in 1683 as one of the hundreds of "Seven Years Passengers" who arrived regularly to be sold into servitude. This was a convenient way for plantation owners, who desperately needed laborers to work their land, to attain the help they needed. The owner of a tobacco plantation located on the Patapsco River in Maryland purchased Molly's labor, and she was put to work in the fields.

In 1690, after serving her seven years on the plantation, Molly was released and given the items that were customary supplied by the employer. Armed with an ox, cart, plow, clothing, gun, and seeds with which to plant crops, Molly staked a claim near the Patapsco River on Cooper's Branch, not far from her former master's plantation. For a few years, she worked the land alone, saving her earnings from Indian corn and tobacco harvests. Though she was opposed to slavery, she needed help on the farm.

Money in hand, she traveled to the docks and bought two slaves from a ship that had recently arrived from Africa. One of the slaves, whose name is not known, was robust and hardworking. The other was Bannaka, a frail individual who claimed to be the son of an African king. In Silvio A. Bedini's *The Life of Benjamin Banneker* (1999), Bannaka is described as being "a man of bright intelligence, fine temper, with a very agreeable presence, dignified manners, and contemplative habits." Molly grew to love Bannaka, and he returned her love. After freeing Bannaka (as well as the other slave), Molly ignored the law against mixed-race marriages and married him, taking his name as her surname.

integrated system of complex (for the times) mechanical hardware, including a waterwheel. As always, Banneker's fascination with mechanics was in the forefront of his daily life. Drawn by its mechanisms, he frequented the mill enough to become friends with the Ellicotts. In this way, the arrival of the mill became the first real link for the solitary Banneker to the budding world of technology. The area later became known as Ellicott Mills.

Among the Ellicott family was 12-year-old George, son of one of the brothers. George shared Banneker's fascination with science, and while there was a generation gap of 29 years between them, they still became good friends.

It was George Ellicott who first became interested in astronomy, and he had the means to pursue it. He began to acquire textbooks and instruments imported from England, including a celestial globe and various telescopes. Banneker was right there with him, learning along with George at an insatiable rate. In this way, George was the key influence in Banneker's becoming involved with astronomy.

At Age 57, Banneker Tackles Astronomy

By 1788, Banneker's scientific interest bent toward astronomy in such a way that George could not keep the man satisfied. The subject fascinated Banneker more than anything else in his life. It was not long before George arrived at Banneker's farm with books and instruments, including a pedestal telescope, a sturdy table on which to rest it, and a set of drafting instruments for making astronomical observations. One of the first books Banneker read was James Ferguson's *An Easy Introduction to Astronomy for Young Gentlemen and Ladies* (1768). He also studied a more detailed and complex book called *Mayer's Lunar Tables* (1753) by the German cartographer and astronomer Johann Tobias Mayer, another self-taught mathematician. Also among his new and modest library was Charles Leadbetter's *A Complete System of Astronomy* (1742), the most comprehensive and advanced book of his collection.

Due to George's busy schedule, he did not have time to instruct Banneker. Once again, Banneker was forced to educate himself. He had no problem with that. Beginning in 1789, after carefully reading each of his books, Banneker turned to his telescope and put to work what he had learned. Each night, for hours on end, he would make observations. Astronomy had taken hold of him in a way that overshadowed his other responsibilities to the extent that the farm began to suffer. He felt guilty for his neglect of the land, yet he could not tear himself away from his new fascination. His life had found new meaning. Aside from his friend George Ellicott, Banneker was involved in something no one else grasped, and this gave him enormous pleasure.

From Farmer to Astronomer

After tending his crops for the day, Banneker would eagerly turn to his astronomy. He soon began to keep a manuscript journal of his calculations on the projection of eclipses and other astronomical predictions. He always shared his work with George, seeking approval on his projections from the man he considered his vast superior in the subject. Banneker's aptitude for astronomy never failed to impress George, stimulating Banneker's confidence in his own abilities as an astronomer. He began to consider preparing his own ephemeris, which led to the idea that he might even be able to compile his own almanac. He dared not to think about whether the finished product could be publishable material, but he set that doubt in the back of his mind, and in early 1790, he began to construct his tables.

Brilliant Creation and Blinding Disappointment

When Banneker set out to write an almanac—a book few households were without—no African American had ever done so. It was a challenge, but Banneker had never shrunk from a challenge. He was a free man and as such he was capable of doing anything he set his mind to.

Banneker went to work on the ephemeris, almost unable to stop himself. By this time, his mother, Mary, had died, and he was the sole caretaker of the farm and all the duties it demanded. During the first half of 1790, he spent long hours organizing data and compiled an ephemeris for 1791 while still tending to the farm and household chores. As the new year approached, time was of the essence, as his faithful wooden clock reminded him each time it struck the hour. The manuscript needed to be ready to send to a prospective publisher in time to be printed for the next year, if indeed it would be printed at all.

At last it was complete. The ephemeris was a magnificent amount of work, carefully copied onto the finest pages he could afford, in the format consistent with an almanac. Convinced his

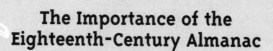

The Importance of the Eighteenth-Century Almanac

The importance of an almanac during this period should not be underestimated. Since its introduction to the American colonies in 1639, printed material available to the rural public was usually restricted to two books: the almanac and the Bible. The almanac was a cherished possession for any household and basically served as the only calendar available. (The common household calendar really did not come into regular print and regular use until late in the 19th century.) Each year, a new almanac was produced for the coming year and was available for purchase before the start of that year.

The first almanacs consisted only of an ephemeris, which served the user in calculating the rising and setting of the Sun and key stars. A navigator would use it to determine his position from certain fixed stars and predict the tides. The farmer would use the celestial predictions in order to know when to plow the soil, plant, and harvest his crops by the phases of the Moon, and when to expect the summer solstice or the winter equinox. Around Banneker's time, it gradually began offering additional material, such as weather predictions, histories, astrology, dates of special events, and even poetry.

The *Old Farmer's Almanac* is still in publication today. It contains all the classic information plus recipes and cooking tips, gardening tips, and old-fashioned techniques for daily living, such as how to determine the outside temperature by counting the chirps of a cricket. Many people still subscribe to it on a yearly basis and would not think of being without one.

BANNEKER'S EPHEMERIS

1792

June Sixth Month Hath 30 Days

			D	☉	Planets Places ♄	♃	♂	♀	☿	☽
Full ○	4..7..55	Aft		♊	♈	♎	♍	♉	♉	Lat.
Last Q.	11..1..10	Aft	1	11	28	22	24	24	19	2 N
New ☽	19..7..49	Morn	7	17	29	22	26	♊ 1	25	5 N
First Q.	27..5..10	Morn	13	23	♉ 0	22	29	8	♊ 0	2 S
☊ { 1	♍ 30	Deg.	19	29	1	22	♎ 0	16	9	5 S
11	♍ 29	Deg.	25	♋ 4	1	22	2	24	17	1 S
21	♍ 29	Deg.								

M D	W D	Remarkable Days Aspects Weather		☉ Rise	☉ Sets	☽ Long	☽ Sets	☽ South	☽ Age
1	6		warm	4..43	7..17	6..27..6	14..57	9..28	12
2	7		weather	4..42	7..18	7..10.56	15..39	10..20	13
3	G	Trinity Sunday		4..42	7..18	7..25..4	☌	11..17	14
4	2		some	4..41	7..19	8..9..25	rise	12..16	15
5	3	Spica ♍ Sets 1..47	appearance	4..41	7..19	8..24..2	8..18	13..15	16
6	4		rain	4..41	7..19	9..8..46	9..17	14..24	17
7	5			4..40	7..20	9..23..26	10..12	14..12	18
8	6	◁ ♀ ☿	Sultry	4..40	7..20	10..8..2	10..56	16..8	19
9	7		hot	4..40	7..20	10..22..31	11..40	17..2	20
10	G	1st Sunday after Trinity	weather	4..39	7..21	11..6..45	12..18	17.54	21
11	2	St. Barnabas		4..39	7..21	1..20..39	12..49	18..42	22
12	3	◁ ☉ ♃	moderate	4..39	7..21	0..4..15	13..23	19..30	23
13	4	☿ great elongation 22°.53'	gentle	4..39	7..21	0..7..26	14..1	20..18	24
14	5		breezes	4..39	7..21	1..0..22	14..35	21..6	25
15	6	Pegasi Markab rise 10..32		4..38	7..22	1..13..1	15..8	21..53	26
16	7			4..38	7..22	1..25..24	15..48	22..40	27
17	G	2nd Sunday after Trinity St. Alban		4..38	7..22	2..7..32	16..27	23..27	28
18	2			4..38	7..22	2..19..30	♂	♂	29
19	3	Days 14..44	cloudy	4..38	7..22	3..1..34	Sets	0..14	☽
20	4	☉ enters ♋	and like	4..38	7..22	3..13..15	7..38	0..55	1
21	5	Longest Day	for	4..38	7..22	3..25..4	8..40	1..44	2
22	6		rain	4..38	7..22	4..7..0	9..30	2..38	3
23	7	◁ ♃ ♀		4..38	7..22	4..19..2	10..6	3..25	4
24	G	3rd Sunday after Trinity St. John Bap.		4..38	7..22	5..1..13	10.36	4..5	5
25	2			4..38	7..22	5..13..39	11..7	4..50	6
26	3		thunder	4..38	7..22	5..26..19	11..41	5..34	7
27	4	♃ Sets 1..2	gusts	4..38	7..22	6..9..20	12..12	6..22	8
28	5		and rain	4..38	7..22	6..22..40	12..48	7..12	9
29	6	St. Peter and Paul	toward	4..39	7..21	7..6..7	13..22	8..3	10
30	7	Days Decrease 2 m	the end	4..39	7..21	7..20..16	14..10	8..58	11

Reproduction of a page from Banneker's astronomical journal. The original manuscript now resides in the collections of the Maryland Historical Society.

astronomical tables were of his best work, Banneker sent it to Goddard and Angell, a prominent publisher in Baltimore. To his grave disappointment, his manuscript was promptly rejected. He tried another and met with the same result. His third try was with Goddard's rival, John Hays. As it so happened, Hays was the publisher for the renowned surveyor Major Andrew Ellicott, cousin to Banneker's close friend George. Major Ellicott, then living in Philadelphia, was himself author of several almanacs published within the last few years. Hays reported to Banneker that he might be willing to publish his 1791 ephemeris if the work was of acceptable quality. With that said, Hays sent Banneker's manuscript to Major Ellicott for his inspection. When at last Hays finally declined to publish Banneker's work, attesting that his readers were used to the Ellicott almanac and would not welcome a different author, it was too late for him to try and find a new publisher in time for the almanac to be ready for 1791. Banneker was devastated, and he retreated to his farmhouse in bitter disappointment.

Fate Lends a Hand

When his luck seemed the bleakest and his faith in his own ability began to suffer, fate stepped in to lend Banneker a hand. During the past few years, an antislavery movement had begun. The slave trade had been abolished in a December 1774 congressional resolution that allowed for no more importation or purchase of slaves. Also, an organization existed called the Society for the Relief of Free Negroes, to which prominent public figures such as Benjamin Rush (ca. 1745–1813), and James Pemberton (1723–1809) belonged. The society's goal was to gather evidence that blacks were not an inferior race and to free them from slavery.

In October 1790, Major Ellicott handed to James Pemberton a letter Banneker had written to him when Hays was still pondering the idea of publishing the ephemeris of a black man. Banneker's letter addressed both his concerns and confidences about his own work and asked the major for any help he might be able to lend to his research. Pemberton immediately saw the importance that Banneker's work as a free black man could mean to the society, and to African Americans as a whole. Banneker's astronomical work was hard evidence that the African intellect was equal to anyone's. He forwarded a copy of Banneker's letter to Joseph Townsend of the Baltimore chapter of the society, who in turn sought out the publisher John Hays to inquire as to the details of Banneker's work. Banneker now seemed to have the backing he needed to publish his almanac. It was too late in the year, however, for his 1791 tables to print. Banneker would have to compile a new set of tables for 1792.

An Unexpected Turn of Events

Early in 1791, Banneker had an unexpected personal visit from Major Ellicott. A location had been established for a new seat of government. Both Maryland and Virginia had surrendered large tracts of land to serve as the new federal territory. Under the direct employ of George Washington, the first president of the United States, the major was quickly recruiting help in the survey of the land. Work was soon to begin on what, when finished, would be called the District of Columbia (Washington, D.C.). Major Elliott wanted Banneker on the team to assist him in the surveyor's observatory tent. Banneker was overcome with excitement, especially at the thought of getting to see and perhaps use the major's surveying instruments, such as his *transit* and equal altitude instrument, the large *zenith* sector, and his astronomical clock.

Flattered at the major's confidence in him, Banneker readily agreed, and arrangements were made for his sisters, who lived nearby, to look after the farm. He was soon on his way, mounted on horseback beside the major, taking with him a gentlemen's wardrobe provided by George's wife, Elizabeth Ellicott.

When the trip was over, Banneker found himself in Alexandria, Virginia, where the major set up his base camp and astronomical tent. Banneker's job, though he was untrained in the art of surveying, was to serve as Major Ellicott's assistant. He maintained notes, made calculations, and used the astronomical instruments to establish base points of the area. He was kept so busy that he took up residence right in the astronomical tent. In his spare time, he worked on his 1792 ephemeris.

Yet Banneker was no longer a young man. He was 60 years old. Due to the extremes of the climate, to which he was unaccustomed, and his fondness for strong drink, Banneker's health was beginning to degenerate. Though he fully enjoyed the work and the company of the men, after just four months on the job, Banneker decided to return to his farm to rest and work on his almanac.

His First Almanac

Banneker had learned a great deal about astronomy from Major Ellicott. He put this knowledge to work as he compiled his new ephemeris. In June 1791, two months after his return home, Banneker finished the first draft of his 1792 almanac. He took his work to two printers, Goddard and Angell in Baltimore and Crukshank and Humpreys in Philadelphia, both of whom ultimately acknowledged that Banneker's work was of the highest competence and agreed to publish his work. As Banneker had hoped, Joseph Pemberton and the Society for the Relief of Free Negroes played a significant role in supporting Banneker in view of the publishers. According to S. A. Bedini's *Benjamin Banneker*, on a morning in late December 1791, an advertisement in the Baltimore paper read:

> Benjamin Banneker's highly approved Almanac, for 1792, to be sold by the Printers hereof, Wholesale and Retail.

Banneker could not have been happier or more grateful to his friends. He had received personal support from a number of prominent figures, the Ellicott family being chief among them, including the now famous geographer general of the United States, Major Andrew Ellicott. In the end, however, it was not who he knew that caused his almanac to succeed, but the fine work of the almanac itself.

After negotiations between the printers were finalized, his 1792 almanac was printed by Goddard and Angell in Baltimore (the same publisher who rejected his first almanac), by Crukshank and Humphreys in Philadelphia, and by Hanson and Bond in Alexandria. This was a historical first in major scientific accomplishments by African Americans and was a key event in the advocacy of the abolition of slavery. Through his work, Banneker proved that the intellect of an African was equal to any.

The Last Years

Banneker's first almanac was a success, and he published one each year thereafter until 1797. In his 1793 almanac, Banneker included an August 1791 correspondence between himself and then secretary of state Thomas Jefferson. Banneker tactfully challenged Jefferson's stance that blacks possessed an inferior intellect by providing for the secretary a copy of his ephemeris with his letter. Jefferson's reply was in praise of Banneker's accomplishments in science.

In his later years, Banneker's health continued to suffer. Eventually, his farm fell into disrepair as advanced old age set in. He was an old man alone, and persons known and unknown began to harass him. He had decided to rent out his land for others to work, but the arrangements were tenuous. Renters failed to pay. Personal belongings or livestock would go missing. Shots would sometimes ring out against his farmhouse from unknown origins in the bushes. Individuals whom Banneker refused to name, fearing retribution, made threats on his life. His home was burglarized. His fruit trees were stripped.

Banneker had been parceling out his land since 1791, but soon he tired of trying to pry money from the renters, so he sold a significant portion of it to the Ellicotts under the condition that he stay in residence at the farmhouse with his garden until the day of his death. Other neighbors bought out the rest, until finally, in 1799, while lying quite ill in bed, Banneker transferred the remainder of his land to the Ellicotts.

In his retirement and until the day of his death, Banneker spent the nights awake, observing the stars, leaving much of the daylight hours for sleeping. The last day of his life occurred on a clear autumn morning. On October 9, 1806, Banneker was out walking as usual, when he came upon an acquaintance. The two talked for a while, but soon Banneker admitted that he did not feel well. He and the friend walked back to the farmhouse, where Banneker lay down on his sofa. Not long afterward, the astronomer passed away in his sleep. During his funeral two days later, his house caught fire and burned to the ground. Everything he owned, including his faithful wooden clock, was reduced to ash. Some were convinced the fire was deliberately set.

Even though the man's possessions are gone and little remains to chronicle the life of the self-educated astronomer Benjamin Banneker, his written works endure. Through his astronomical works, Banneker proved that the capacity for thought was not linked to the color of one's skin. Banneker's contribution to astronomy was a series of almanacs and ephemerides that were the best available in their day.

CHRONOLOGY

1731	Born on November 9 near Baltimore, Maryland
1752	Becomes well known for constructing a handmade wall clock after seeing a pocket watch for the first time
1772	Greatly influenced by the Ellicott family, who have newly moved to the area
1788	Receives loans of books and instruments on astronomy from George Ellicott
1789	Begins making astronomical observations
1790	Constructs his own ephemeris with the intent to publish an almanac. The manuscript is rejected until the Society for the Relief of Free Negroes becomes involved.
1791	Learns he must compile a new ephemeris to publish in 1792. He is offered a job assisting in the survey of the District of Columbia. Writes a letter to Thomas Jefferson addressing his hypocrisy toward blacks
1792–97	His first 1792 almanac is published in Baltimore, Philadelphia, and Alexandria. He will produce one each year for the next five years.
1806	Dies on the morning of October 9 after a morning walk

FURTHER READING

Books

Bedini, Silvio A. *The Life of Benjamin Banneker.* 2d ed. Baltimore: Maryland Historical Society, 1999. A very well-researched and updated account of Benjamin Banneker's life, his scientific achievements, the influence of the people around him, and the obstacles he surmounted as a minority.

Cerami, Charles, and Robert M. Silverstein. *Benjamin Banneker: Surveyor, Astronomer, Publisher, Patriot.* Hoboken, N.J.: John Wiley & Sons, 2002. A highly detailed version of Benjamin Banneker's life that explores the true genius of this self-educated 18th-century astronomer.

Conley, Kevin, and Nathan Irvin Huggins. *Benjamin Banneker: Scientist and Mathematician (Black Americans of Achievement).* Langhorne, Pa.: Chelsea House Publishers, 1989. A complete biography of Benjamin Banneker with photographs and illustrative material, written for middle school readers and up.

Litwin, Laura Baskes. *Benjamin Banneker: Astronomer and Mathematician (African-American Biographies).* Berkeley Heights, N.J.: Enslow Publishers, 1999. A superior work written in easy language that reviews the highlights of Benjamin Banneker's life.

Wadsworth, Ginger. *Benjamin Banneker: Pioneering Scientist.* Minneapolis: Carolrhoda Books, 2003. A well-written book portraying the self-educated scientist Benjamin Banneker as an excellent role model for young people. Includes color illustrations.

Web Sites

Brown, Mitchell. "Benjamin Banneker. The Faces of Science: African American in Science." Princeton University. Available online. URL: http://www.princeton.edu/~mcbrown/display/banneker.html. Accessed November 29, 2004. A biography of Benjamin Banneker that includes a lengthy bibliography and links to related sites.

Williams, Scott W. "Mathematicians of the African Diaspora: Benjamin Banneker." State University of New York at Buffalo. Available online. URL: http://www.math.buffalo.edu/mad/special/banneker-benjamin.html. Accessed November 29, 2004. This Web site offers a brief history of Benjamin Banneker and provides links to other sites related to African Americans important to the contemporary history of science and mathematics.

6

Sir William Herschel

(1738–1822)

Sir William Herschel used his superior mirror designs and a new methodical system of measurement to discover the approximate shape of the Milky Way, and revealed that it was in motion. *(Photo courtesy of the Library of Congress)*

The Father of Sidereal Astronomy

The German-born English astronomer Sir William Herschel is considered the father of *sidereal* astronomy. In other words, he was the first person to systematically study the stars and their attributes. After designing and building the most superior telescopes and instruments of his time, he discovered the planet Uranus, the seventh planet of our solar system. He observed and mapped many celestial objects and correctly discovered numerous astronomical facts, including the proper motion of the Sun and solar system. He also determined that most double stars were actually *binary*, revealed the correct shape of the Milky Way, cataloged thousands of *nebulae*, and proposed the idea that some of the nebulae existed beyond the Milky Way and were galaxies of stars on their own.

In the Footsteps of His Father

Friedrich Wilhelm Herschel was born on November 15, 1738, in Hanover, Germany, to Isaac Herschel and Anna Ilse Mortizen. His father, a passionate musician since his youth, was a career musician in the Hanoverian Guard band. His mother was in charge of raising the six children and had distaste for advanced learning, claiming it was the root of all problems.

Fortunately for the four young Herschel boys, their father took charge of their educations. The two Herschel girls were not so fortunate, and due to the insistence of their mother, were doomed to a childhood of learning nothing outside of tending to household chores.

As the boys grew up, they attended the public school and were also taught music privately at home by their father. Besides music, their father also had a fond appreciation of astronomy, which is where young Wilhelm gained his first spark of interest in the subject. He proved to be an exceptional pupil at home and at school, especially in mathematics and mechanics, and enjoyed deep, idealistic discussions with his father. By the time he was 14 years old, he was accomplished enough on a variety of instruments to become a member of the Hanoverian Guard band, along with his elder brother Jacob.

An Escape to England

In 1757, there was a French invasion at Hanover, and the Hanoverian Guard became caught up in actual battle. Herschel's health had never been the best, and the conditions of warfare took their toll on him. His parents intervened and, in 1757, arranged for Herschel to escape into England.

Caroline Herschel

Sir William Herschel's younger sister Caroline Lucretia Herschel was born on March 16, 1750, in Hanover, Germany. Growing up, Caroline had always been told that her looks were so plain that she should expect no suitors and to look forward to many years living at home helping her mother. Early in life, Caroline displayed the same aptitude for learning as William, but her mother forbade her and her older sister, Sophia, any kind of formal education. Despite her father's occasional attempts to satisfy her intellectual interests, Caroline's mother controlled her life, which was mostly filled with knitting, washing, and dusting.

In 1772, Caroline's luck changed, in the form of a job offer choreographed by her brother William, who was then working as a professional musician in England. After winning a battle with her mother over whether or not she could leave, Caroline joined William in Bath and was introduced not only to singing lessons, but also to the fascinating world

Herschel changed his name from Wilhelm to William and made a living around Yorkshire through his music. In his spare time, he continued with his interest in mathematics and mechanics, which included astronomy.

In 1765, he became the organist at the Halifax Parish Church, and one year later he took a job in Bath, England, as an organist for the Octagon Chapel. Herschel was very fond of his younger sister Caroline and felt pity for her life of drudgery and housework. When the soprano in Herschel's orchestra quit, he quickly suggested his sister Caroline for the position, a decision that would ultimately bring about the first appointment of a woman astronomer to the Royal Society of London.

of mathematics. She began to study algebra, geometry, and trigonometry, and was also introduced to her brother's part-time obsession, which was astronomy.

Between musical performances, Caroline was soon assisting her brother in his astronomical studies. On August 1, 1786, she discovered her first comet, which brought her public recognition as an astronomical observer. After that, her reputation as an astronomer continued to grow, and in 1787, King George III granted her a yearly salary of £50 for her role as assistant to her brother Sir William Herschel, the king's astronomer.

Between 1786 and 1797, she discovered eight more comets and was the first to index a star catalog by English astronomer John Flamsteed (1646–1719). She later contributed to the education of William Herschel's son, John, who himself became a significant astronomer. In 1828, Caroline was awarded the gold medal of the Royal Astronomical Society and in 1835 she and the Scottish mathematician, naturalist, and mineralogist Mary Somerville (1780–1872) were the first women ever to be elected to the prestigious Royal Society of London.

Herschel Refines the Art of Optic-making

In 1772, around the time his sister Caroline joined him in England, Herschel had recently experienced his first view of the stars through an inferior telescope. This was a life-changing event for him, and he became very excited at the thought of peering at the stars more closely through a better instrument. He first tried renting a *reflecting* telescope and, though it was the best he could find, it was still quite inadequate where he was concerned. Herschel decided there was only one thing to do. He would create a reflecting telescope himself. He had done some study on optics, but not enough. He needed to learn more.

Herschel set to work learning how to grind and polish his own mirrors, which in those days were usually made of highly polished metal, not glass like today's models. By this time, his brother Alexander, also a musician, had arrived in Bath. With the help of both Caroline and Alexander, Herschel cast and polished a number of mirrors until, in 1773, he finally completed his first reflecting telescope. It had a seven-foot (2.1 m) length and a six-inch (15 cm) mirror and was the best to be had in all England and undoubtedly in the entire world. His experiments with optics resulted in the improvement over any other telescope in existence.

Month after month, he worked on hundreds of mirrors, experimenting with different methods to cast and polish *reflectors*. Finally Herschel tried something no one else had attempted. He increased the copper content in the metal alloys used to cast the mirrors. The reflective quality of the new surfaces became greatly enhanced. Now Herschel could clearly make out celestial objects that, before, were little more than fuzzy spots in the eyepiece. In 1774, he clearly observed the Orion Nebula.

Sir William Herschel ground more than 200 lenses over the course of a few months in order to discover the best means to cast and polish a superior mirror. This is an original pair of mirrors he developed. They are made from speculum metal, a highly tarnishable material used extensively in mirror making of all kinds in the early 1800s. Today, modern mirrors are made from aluminum coating on special low thermal expansion glass. *(Photo by Larry Adkins/Courtesy of the Science Museum, London/Science and Society Picture Library)*

A Monumental Discovery

During the next few years, Herschel continued to practice building telescopes. He also began systematically mapping the night sky
and recording his findings. He compiled papers on sunspots, vari-
able stars, the geography of the Moon, and the poles of Mars. This
was all significant work, but in 1781, Herschel made a monumen-
tal discovery.

On the night of March 13, 1781, as Herschel was observing with
his favorite seven-foot telescope, he noticed a strange object in the
constellation of Gemini that had the distinct shape of a solid disk.
Its dim light did not glimmer and flicker like a star, but remained
steady and true, like the reflected light of a planet. He was not quite
sure what to make of it, yet he knew he needed to make a decision
as to its nature and announce his find.

Herschel decided to announce his discovery as a new comet. This
news caused a stampede of other astronomers to their instruments
in order to verify the new celestial event. Yet, as Herschel continued
to observe, it became clear to him, and eventually to other
astronomers, that the object's behavior indeed appeared to be consistent with the behavior of a planet. It had a defined edge like a
planet, and its nearly circular orbital motions were in harmony with
those of the other established planets. Comets were known to have
very elliptical orbits, not circular. After using parallax measurements, he also found that the new object was far beyond Saturn, the
sixth (counting Earth) and farthest planet at edge of the known solar
system. Eventually, it was officially determined that Herschel's discovery was indeed a new planet, one that existed at roughly twice
the distance from the Sun as Saturn! This tore a great rift in the
ancient knowledge that defined the size of the solar system based on
the placement of the six planets. The discovery of this seventh planet nearly doubled the size of the solar system. This was fascinating
news! Suddenly the telescope was again popular in a way not seen
since Galileo discovered the moons of Jupiter in 1610.

The King's Astronomer

The discovery of the new planet made Herschel an instant celebrity. He named the planet Georgium Sidus, in honor of King George

Telescope Building at Home

It is quite possible to build a telescope at home today. It is not difficult, yet it does take some patience. Looking at the stars and planets through a device created by oneself is a true pleasure, and anyone with the time and a little spending money can do it. Kits from hobby stores provide most of the materials needed to begin a telescope-building project, and the prices vary depending on the size of telescope one wants. The most popular size for the beginner is the six-inch (15 cm) reflecting telescope. "Six inches" refers to the diameter of the mirror, not the length of the tube.

An important part of telescope creation is in the grinding of the mirror. Like most worthwhile things, precision accuracy can be accomplished with practice using simple equipment and one's own two hands. All that is needed for grinding is a solid support stand at about waist level, water, grinding abrasive, and two glass discs, one of which is called the mirror blank and the other, the tool.

Placing the blank atop the tool, with the center of the blank near the edge of the tool and a wet abrasive in between, one begins to grind by rubbing the two together in a circular motion while also walking around the stand to insure uniformity. As one does this, the top blank will become concave and the bottom tool will become convex. As work progresses, finer and finer abrasive powder is used, making the surface increasingly smoother. Examples of some abrasives are silicone carbide, emery, and aluminum oxide. Upon completion, the surfaces will be highly reflective. Many hours of grinding and changing grit from coarse to fine are required to prepare a mirror surface. Simple tests on reflectivity and *focal length* can be achieved by using an ordinary lightbulb or sunlight and some glycerin.

III, and the name remained such all of Herschel's life. (In 1850 it was officially renamed Uranus, after the father of Saturn—a fitting new name since Saturn was the father of Jupiter and Jupiter was the father of Mars, in that order.) Due to his discovery, in 1781 Herschel became a member of the Royal Society of London.

King George III heard of Herschel's achievement and summoned him to court. Duly impressed, the king offered Herschel a position as royal astronomer with a salary of £200 a year. This enabled Herschel to end his musical career and devote all of his time to astronomy. In time, Caroline was also employed, earning £50 a year as assistant to the new royal astronomer. In 1782, they both moved to Datchet, Berkshire, to begin their new roles in astronomy. By 1784, William Herschel had compiled a catalog of 800 double stars, arriving at the conclusion that many were not double stars at all, but were in fact binary stars, which are two stars that rotate around a common center of mass. Double stars are two stars that appear close in the sky but have no physical connection. Herschel's conclusion of the motion of binary stars was the first hard evidence in support of Newton's universal law of gravitation (named for Sir Isaac Newton, who first proposed such a law in 1687).

Herschel also went to work on plans for a bigger, 30-foot (9 m) telescope, but his plans were canceled. The metal cast for the mirror would have weighed 500 pounds (227 kg)! It was not something easily handled, and he did not have the means to do it. This did not stop him. In 1786, after he and Caroline moved to Slough, where observing was better, Herschel announced a plan to construct a great 40-foot (12.2 m) telescope with a 48-inch (122 cm) mirror. King George backed him with the necessary financing and labor. For the grinding of such an enormous mirror, Herschel designed a special device.

By 1787, while still working on his 48-inch telescope, Herschel discovered two moons orbiting Uranus, using another telescope of his creation, a 20-inch (61 cm) reflecting telescope. In 1788, he married the widow of a wealthy merchant, Mary Baldwin Pitt. Together they had a son, John Frederick William Herschel (1792–1871), who also became an astronomer. The moons of Uranus were later given names by his son John: Titania and Oberon.

The great telescope was finished in 1789 and erected inside a huge wooden framework. Herschel's telescopes strayed from the common design of the Newtonian reflecting telescope (developed

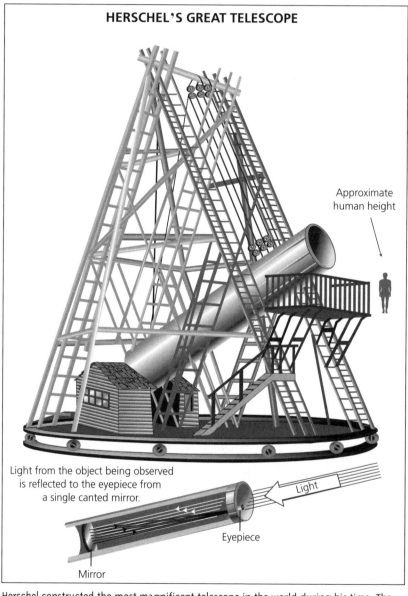

HERSCHEL'S GREAT TELESCOPE

Approximate human height

Light from the object being observed is reflected to the eyepiece from a single canted mirror.

Light

Eyepiece

Mirror

Herschel constructed the most magnificent telescope in the world during his time. The device was 40 feet (12.2 m) long with a 48-inch (122 cm) mirror. He stood on a scaffold near the lip of the telescope in order to see into the eyepiece.

by Isaac Newton in 1668) because the primary mirror was slanted in a way that threw the image to the side, where it could be viewed near the lip of the opening. This design was called the Herschelian telescope, and it required no secondary mirror, which meant less grinding. Unfortunately, for viewing to take place, Herschel had to climb a scaffold high off the ground in order to look into the top of the instrument. Though Herschel's mirror design was unique, large telescopes were common, and more than a few persons were known to have fallen from the framework while observing the night sky.

Through the new great telescope, he at once discovered two new moons of Saturn, bringing its number of moons up to seven. With some dismay, however, Herschel found that the best instrument of his creation was his smaller 20-inch telescope and the cumbersome, 40-foot instrument was used only seldom. The drawback to all Herschel's (and most other) telescopes was the constant need to remove the metal mirrors and polish away the tarnish. This time-consuming task was also done more quickly and easily with the smaller telescope.

The Shaping of the Galaxy

Through his work on binary stars, Herschel proved that stars, not just planets, had motion. This was significant data, considering that until that time, stars were regarded as fixed objects in the *celestial sphere*. Herschel began to ask himself if the Sun in our own solar system was on the move, which he showed was precisely the case.

Using his superior instruments, Herschel was able to determine the stars' proper motion. He determined that in one part of the sky, the stars seemed to be moving away from one another, and stars in the opposite part of the sky seemed to be moving together. He suggested that the Sun was in motion with the stars that seemed to be moving away, and he also indicated the direction in which the entire galaxy was moving. This was another scientific discovery that rocked the core of ancient belief that the solar system, hence humankind, was the absolute center of the universe. If the Sun were in motion, then around what did it revolve? Where was the center of the universe, if a center truly even existed? It was finally decided

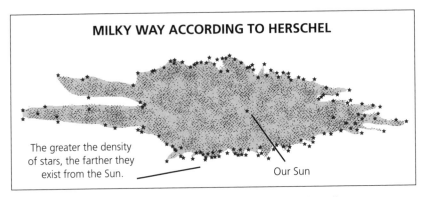

This is a reproduction of Herschel's rendering of the structure of the Milky Way according to his disc theory, which appeared in his paper "On the Construction of the Heaven," published in 1785.

that the Sun and our solar system were in motion near the center of the universe, and that was still close enough for most people's perception of a divine design.

Herschel went further with his studies by inventing a systematic method that counted the number of stars in selected areas of the sky in order to determine the shape of the Milky Way. After compiling extensive data, he proposed a number for the amount of stars in the Milky Way, which was around 300 million. He also stated that its shape was like that of a wispy pancake, with a diameter four times its thickness. He applied this same disc-with-tendrils shape to similar celestial objects that appeared remote, which came to be known as *galaxies*, the Greek word for Milky Way. In this way, Herschel was the first to scientifically verify the existence and overall shape of galaxies.

Herschel also made observations of the Sun and kept a log. Between 1779 and 1806, he recorded his observations and devised his own unique terminology for his discoveries, such as the word *openings* for sunspots. He also confirmed that the Sun was gaseous in nature.

In 1800, as a result of his solar observations, he became the first to detect the existence of infrared radiation. Initially, he was merely curious about the various temperatures produced as sunlight passed through the different colored filters he used to observe the Sun. By experimenting with a prism that divided light into all known spectrums, Herschel discovered that the highest temperature in the spectrum of visible light came from the red spectrum. Using a thermometer with a blackened tip, he investigated further and found that a form of invisible light (radiation) existed beyond the visible red spectrum, made evident by the continued rise in temperature where apparently no light existed beyond red. Through these experiments with light spectrums and their individual heat readings, Herschel was the first to record the existence of "light," or electromagnetic radiation, beyond visible light. This energy would later come to be known as infrared light.

By 1802, Herschel finished a 16-year-long study on nebulae. He recorded 2,514 nebulae and was the first to identify many of them as being heavy clusters of stars rather than just dust clouds, and that some were perhaps distant galaxies. In his papers, he touched on a theory of stellar evolution by proposing that the universe began as nebulous clouds. He hypothesized that these nebulae gradually gathered into varying gravitational masses that over time evolved into separate star clusters. He theorized that through collapse of some of these clusters, new nebulae would form and split away as newborn diffuse clouds, and then the process would begin again.

A Knight's Tale

Throughout his productive life, Hershel compiled and published numerous papers, ranging from the first discovery of Uranus in 1781 to an 1821 catalog of 145 double stars. In 1816, the prince of Wales, George IV, knighted Herschel, and in 1820 the Royal Astronomical Society was founded, of which Herschel was appointed president in 1821.

During his time, Herschel was a leader in his field. The achievements of other astronomers paled in comparison, since by no other means in the history of the Earth had a human being served as witness to the secrets harbored in such far reaches of the heavens. Not only had he discovered the first new planet since ancient history, Herschel could proudly claim that he had looked farther into the universe than any before him. With his improved telescope, he made pioneering observations and contributed irrefutable new data to human understanding of the universe. On August 25, 1822, Herschel died in his home on Windsor Road (known as Observatory House) in Slough, England.

Before he died, Sir William Herschel's pioneering achievements of observation and measurement significantly advanced the science of astronomy and made him the most skilled astronomer of 18th-century Europe.

CHRONOLOGY

1738	Born on November 15 in Hanover, Germany
1752	Becomes a member of the Hanoverian Guard band
1757	Escapes to England to avoid war
1766	Takes a position in Bath, England, as an organist for the Octagon Chapel
1772	First views the stars through a low-resolution telescope, igniting interest in developing better observational equipment
1773	Builds his first telescope with optics and mirrors produced by his own hand
1774	Discovers the Orion Nebula with his improved telescope and begins to map the heavens
1781	Revolutionizes conception of the solar system by discovering a new planet, later named Uranus; becomes a member of the Royal Society
1782	Appointed as royal astronomer; sister Caroline is named assistant astronomer
1784	Concludes that many double stars are actually binary stars, which adds direct support to Newton's universal law of gravitation
1786	Sister Caroline discovers a new comet
1789	Finishes construction on his famous 40-foot (12.2 m) telescope

1792	John Frederick William Herschel, Herschel's son and future astronomer, is born
1800	Discovers infrared light
1802	Finishes a star catalog of more than 2,514 nebulae
1816	Knighted by George IV, prince of Wales
1822	Dies on August 25 in Slough, England

FURTHER READING
Books

Asimov, Isaac. *Eyes on the Universe: A History of the Telescope*. Boston: Houghton Mifflin, 1975. A thoroughly researched book from a popular author about the impact of telescopes, including chapters on Sir William Herschel and his discoveries.

Crawford, Deborah. *The King's Astronomer: Sir William Herschel*. New York: Messner, 2000. A book on Sir William Herschel told in dramatic style that keeps the reader's attention.

Hammond, D. B. *Stories of Scientific Discovery*. Freeport, N.Y.: Books for Libraries Press, 1969. Includes an excellent chapter on Sir William Herschel, plus other entries that further acquaint the reader with the history of astronomy.

Herrmann, Dieter B.; Kevin Krisciunas, translator. *The History of Astronomy from Herschel to Hertzsprung (Geschichte der astronomie von Herschel bis Hertzsprung)*. New York: Cambridge University Press, 1984. Outlines the history of astronomy, detailing influences of Sir William Herschel and other astronomers on the development of astronomy as a science.

Web Sites

Arnett, Bill. "William Herschel's Catalog of Deep Sky Objects." Available online. URL: http://www.seds.org/messier/xtra/similar/herschel.html. Accessed November 25, 2004. A wonderful Web page dedicated entirely to William Herschel and his accomplishments, including links to a complete Herschel directory, biographies, and Astronomical League material.

7

Robert H. Goddard

(1882–1945)

Robert Goddard is known for successfully designing, building, and launching the first liquid-fueled rocket in the world.

The Father of Modern Rocketry and Space Flight

The American physicist Robert H. Goddard is known as the father of modern rocketry and *space* flight. He formed the idea of interplanetary travel years before the first successful flight of a powered aircraft and later became the first man to successfully design, build, and then launch a liquid-fueled rocket. His brave and innovative testing with both liquid and solid fuels in rockets laid the groundwork for the development of orbital satellites, *ballistic* missiles, and the first piloted rocket to the Moon. Scientists still hope to send a piloted space flight to Mars, a lifelong dream of Goddard's. Robert Goddard patented numerous rocket and propulsion designs that remain in use today.

A Boy Surrounded by Creativity

Robert Hutchings Goddard was born on October 5, 1882, in Worcester, Massachusetts. In 1883, he moved with his family to Boston, where his father, Nuham Danford Goddard, became a businessman and a successful inventor. His mother was Fannie Louise Goddard.

As a very young child, Robert was stimulated by his father's love of invention, science, and experimentation. Later, it was a fascination with science fiction stories, in particular H. G. Wells's *War of the Worlds*, that drew his scientific mind toward space travel. Throughout his elementary years, Robert was continually involved with scientific experiments. For example, he tried to jump higher than normal off a fence by first attempting to produce static electricity under his feet through friction generated between the gravel and zinc he had removed from a battery. Robert also conducted experiments on perpetual motion, explored the dynamics of kite flying, and marveled in the uses of magnifying glasses.

Robert was not as healthy as other schoolchildren, and illness frequently kept him home. By the time he was in his teens, he had fallen two years behind his peers in general public education. This brought about a great deal of self-education on Robert's part. He spent many hours at home or in the public library, reading books on chemistry, electricity, the atmosphere, and the elements of the Earth. This study of physical and chemical sciences inspired increasingly more elaborate experiments at home, including an attempt to create diamond out of graphite, water, and an oxyhydrogen flame, resulting in an explosion. Later, at age 16, he crafted a balloon made of super-heated aluminum and attempted to fill it with hydrogen and fly it through the air.

While he was in his early teens, Robert's mother fell ill with tuberculosis, and the doctors recommended a change in climate. In 1898, the Goddard family moved back to the open countryside near

Worcester, which was fortuitous for Robert's future experiments in rocketry. The area's broad, flat fields would provide ample room for what would one day become risky launches using dangerous explosive rocket fuels.

After the return to Worcester, Robert read H. G. Wells's *War of the Worlds*, about alien invaders from Mars, which generated in him a sudden burning interest in space travel. He soon had the idea of building and launching his own rocket into space. It was a day Robert would never forget.

The Cherry Tree Incident

One October day in Worcester, shortly after his 17th birthday, Robert was alone in the orchard, intending to do some pruning. Tools in hand, he climbed a cherry tree. As he began to prune, his thoughts wandered. His hands fell idle. H. G. Wells was taking him away again. Then suddenly he had a vision. In his mind's eye, he pictured a mechanical device, one he had never imagined before. It began whirling and whirling, faster and faster, until it lifted from the ground and flew high into the atmosphere. Robert envisioned a vague shape of the vehicle, how it might function, what size it might be at a smaller scale near his feet, and that it could possibly travel all the way to Mars!

Like many sudden, creative inspirations of the human intellect, the thoughts passed quickly through Robert's mind, and soon he was back in the cherry tree, looking at the ground not far below. He smiled. This was something he must try and build! According to Milton Lehman's *Robert H. Goddard: Pioneer of Space Research*, Goddard's diary states that on October 19, 1889, he descended the cherry tree a different person than the one who climbed up. He wrote, "Existence at last seemed very purposive." That day later came to be known to Goddard as "Anniversary Day," the day his life shifted toward the pursuit of space flight.

By 1899, four years before the Wright brothers' first powered flight, Robert confided in one of his close friends about his dream to build a vehicle that could travel out of the atmosphere and through open space to Mars. His friend tried to explain that the laws of physics would deny such an endeavor and that the idea was preposterous.

Robert disagreed, arguing that no physical laws existed against his idea; however, he was at a loss as to where to begin with his grandiose plan. In the meantime, life was marching on. He was becoming a young man and there was his practical future to think about.

The Wrong College

In fall 1900, Goddard enrolled in Becker's Business College in Worcester to learn bookkeeping, an occupation once held by his father. Goddard's mind, though, was bent on his new idea of commanding space flight and it was that, not bookkeeping, which occupied all his thoughts. Time and again, he found himself in the boughs of the cherry tree, dreaming of piloted space flight rather than the dull, regimented life of an office worker. He paid more attention to his experiments in physics than to his class work, which included putting Isaac Newton's third law of motion to the test in his own backyard.

A New Path

By 1901, Robert dropped his courses in bookkeeping and enrolled in Worcester's South High School. His younger classmates received him as something of a phenomenon as he devoured countless books that had anything to do with the hard sciences. Through these years, his enthusiasm for rocketry never faltered. By 1903, he had built small rocket supports and had fired numerous small powder-propelled rockets from his field at home. He even experimented with electronic igniters. In 1904, he graduated as valedictorian from South High and enrolled at Worcester Polytechnic Institute (WPI), a very different path from a future as a humble bookkeeper.

Goddard spent four years at WPI, receiving guidance and special influence from his physics professor, A. Wilmer Duff. During these years, he continued experimenting with small solid-fueled rockets. In 1907, he fired a powder rocket in the basement of the school, causing an explosion, not only in the literal sense, but also his name across the local papers. Rather than expelling Goddard, the school officials took an interest in his work and offered him encouragement.

Isaac Newton's Three Laws of Motion

The English scientist and mathematician Sir Isaac Newton (1643–1727) is considered one of history's greatest scientists. Among many achievements, he is known for the formulation of his law of universal gravitation and of his three laws of motion. In the period 1669–87, he was professor at Cambridge University, the same institution where he received his education. He spent his college years studying the philosophies of such scientific greats as the Greek philosopher Aristotle (384–322 B.C.E.), French philosophers René Descartes (1596–1650) and Pierre Gassendi (1592–1655), English philosopher and political theorist Thomas Hobbes (1588–1679), English natural philosopher and chemist Robert Boyle (1627–91), Italian astronomer and mathematician Galileo Galilei (1564–1642),

Goddard's main problem with the design of a rocket was not in the concept itself; rockets had been around since China invented gunpowder in about 1000 C.E. The problem was devising a practical rocket *propellant* capable of producing enough force to defy the Earth's gravity and reach outer space. This was the problem over which Goddard worried while working to earn his degree.

In 1908, Goddard graduated from WPI with a bachelor's degree in physics. He was a man with one goal: to build a vehicle capable of traveling out of Earth's influence. He immediately entered Clark University in Worcester, one of the first graduate schools in America dedicated to science.

A Russian by the name of Constantine Chikofsky first theorized over the idea of a liquid, rather than black powder, fueled rocket for space travel in an article he published in Russia in 1903. By 1909, Goddard had formulated his own theoretical design for a liquid-fueled rocket using liquid oxygen and liquid hydrogen.

and German astronomer and mathematician Johannes Kepler (1571–1630), as well as many others. The varied influence of all these different scientists developed Newton into a freethinking scientist himself, leading to his founding contributions into many fields of science, including the formulation of his famous three laws of motion:

- Every body continues in its state of rest, or of uniform motion in a straight line, unless it is compelled to change that state by a force impressed on it.
- The change in motion, or rate of change of momentum, is proportional to the motive force impressed and is made in the direction of the straight line in which that force is impressed.
- For every action, there is an equal and opposite reaction.

Newton is also well known for solving mysteries surrounding optics and light, and for helping to found, along with German mathematician Gottfried Wilhelm Leibniz (1646–1716), a new method of mathematics known today as calculus.

Yet so far, all his actual experiments with homemade rocket launching were conducted using products that were readily available, meaning gunpowder. Goddard had more than one design for self-propelled rockets. His list included the cartridge-loading rocket, solar rocket, ionized rocket, liquid hydrogen-oxygen rocket, and even an idea for an atomic rocket. His ideas were grand, but one after another, Goddard found flaws in his conceptual designs, stating they were too expensive or too difficult to carry out. In 1911, Goddard received a doctorate in physics from Clark University.

A Man with a Secret Mission

In 1912, Goddard accepted a research fellowship at Princeton University's Palmer Physical Laboratory. Though the university was supportive to any fresh ideas he wished to pursue, Goddard was reluctant to reveal his rocketry plans. Only in his private time did he work on the physics of propelling mass. During the day at the laboratory, he conducted experiments on displacement currents. In August 1912, Goddard applied for a patent on a charged-particle generator, or an oscillator, an early form of the radio tube. The success of this first patent brought about a degree of confidence to the point that by March 1913, despite a severe bout of tuberculosis that kept him bedridden for much of that year, he began working to prepare a patent application for a rocket propulsion design.

By July 1914, the patent office had issued him two patents. The first, labeled "Rocket Apparatus," was for a multistage rocket. The second, also called "Rocket Apparatus," was for a cartridge-feeding mechanism that introduced successive charges to attain lift, and also included a modification for pumping liquid fuel and an oxidizer into a combustion chamber. In his lifetime, Goddard would eventually be awarded 214 patents in rocketry, 131 of them after his death, most related to liquid-fueled rocket designs and their associated controls components, fuel pumps, motors, and guidance devices. At this stage in his life, though, his beginning designs were theoretical—they had yet to be put to a real test.

In the fall, after recovering from his illness, Goddard declined a further position at Princeton and took a seat as a part-time physics instructor teaching undergraduates at Clark University. He would later go on to become head of the university's physics department and director of its physical laboratories. At Clark University, Goddard was free to create and build in the school's physics shop, expanding the designs of old rockets to accommodate his conceptions of a more powerful means of propulsion. Efficiency was always the rule, for Goddard's experiments were funded entirely from his own pocket.

The de Laval Nozzle

Goddard employed the latest in innovations, including smokeless powders from the Du Pont company. By summer 1915, Goddard had amassed a fine arsenal of varying rockets, concentrating on the

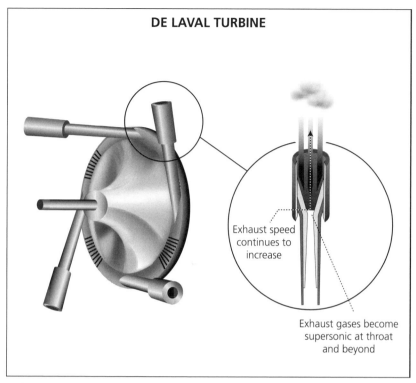

DE LAVAL TURBINE

Exhaust speed
continues to
increase

Exhaust gases become
supersonic at throat
and beyond

Goddard used the tapering nozzle design of Swedish engineer Carl Gustaf de Laval to improve the efficiency of his rocket engines.

most efficient use of different fuels. His experiments showed that upon converting a fuel source to energy, a disappointing 2 percent of the energy from heat was converted to the kinetic energy used to *thrust* the jet. Then he discovered an invention by Swedish engineer Carl Gustaf de Laval, a steam turbine that employed jets of steam to turn wheels. It was the tapering design of the de Laval nozzle that defined an increase in efficiency.

As the steam was forced through an ever-narrowing opening, it sped up. Upon surpassing the speed of sound, the conversion of heat energy to motion became highly efficient. De Laval's nozzle design was just what Goddard needed to increase the performance of his rockets, improving thrust from 2 percent to 40 percent. At this time, Goddard's most successful rocket was a powder-fired rocket that reached an altitude of 486 feet (148 m).

Rockets in Space

There were still questions that, as yet, no one could solve with any certainty. Could thrust be attained in the vacuum of space? Would rocket propellant burn in the absence of oxygen? The answers to these questions were essential to the furthering of space flight. Nearly all physicists said no to both. First, if a rocket had nothing to thrust against, namely atmosphere, it would go nowhere, and second, a rocket propellant would not burn in a vacuum without the presence of oxygen. Goddard knew that propellant compounds carried their own oxygen and in theory were very capable of burning within a vacuum.

To counter the skeptics, he built a vacuum chamber, pumped it empty of air, and mounted a rocket inside. Amazingly, after more than 50 tests, Goddard was able to prove that not only did a rocket work in a vacuum, it achieved roughly 20 percent more thrust than in the atmosphere! Even with this evidence, experts were not convinced, and they treated Goddard as a laughingstock, dismissing his work. This caused the already shy professor to withdraw from public scrutiny. Yet in order to continue, he needed funding; therefore his work would require outside attention if he expected to receive it. He could not keep it a secret and still expect outside sponsorship.

In September 1916, Goddard wrote a letter and sent proof of his work to the secretary of the Smithsonian Institution, asking for financial support in building rocketry capable of high altitudes. The Smithsonian awarded him a grant of $5,000, marking a turning point in Goddard's life and creating jealousy among other scientists. Goddard was able to continue with his experimental rocket designs.

A Career in Rocketry

When the United States entered World War I in 1917, the Army Signal Corps and Ordnance Department solicited Goddard to design a ballistic weapon. By 1918, Goddard and his assistants demonstrated for a military audience various powder-fired guns, later known as bazookas. The war ended before the army could make use of Goddard's designs, and he was all but forgotten by the military.

In 1919, Goddard published a paper through the Smithsonian Miscellaneous Collections titled "A Method of Reaching Extreme

Goddard is shown near Mount Wilson, California, in 1918 as he demonstrates one of his tube-launched rockets, later named the bazooka. *(Photo courtesy of NASA)*

Altitudes," the first document in the United States to cover mathematical theory on the fundamentals of rocket propulsion and the possibility of a space flight that could reach the Moon. In January 1920, the *New York Times* printed an article ridiculing the professor for publicly flaunting such impossible dreams. The article injured Goddard's sensibilities, and he grew even more guarded about his work, revealing details to only a trusted few; however, he continued to seek financing for a liquid-fueled rocket. By now, he was convinced that solid fuels would never be able to produce the thrust required for a rocket to leave the gravitational pull of the Earth and that only through combining liquid oxygen as an accelerant to a fuel of liquid hydrogen could a rocket achieve enough velocity to reach space, his ultimate goal.

By 1920, Goddard was a professor of physics at Clark University (where he remained until 1943) and was living in his lifelong family residence in Worcester. Also in 1920, the U.S. Navy offered him a part-time, confidential rocket development contract. Work would be conducted at a secure facility at the Indian Head Powder Factory in Maryland. This had nothing to do with Goddard's personal goal of producing the first liquid-fueled rocket, but money was money.

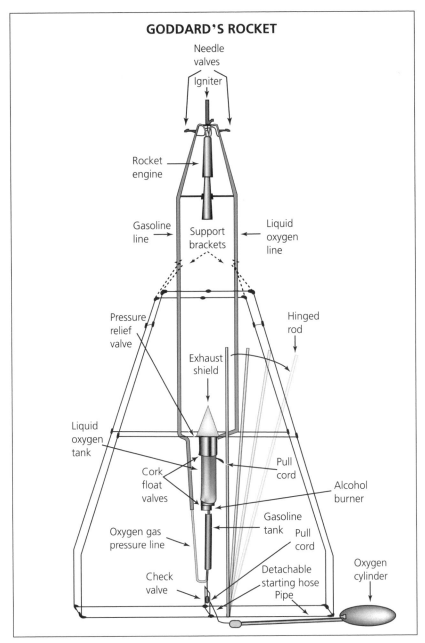

GODDARD'S ROCKET

Needle valves

Igniter

Rocket engine

Gasoline line

Support brackets

Liquid oxygen line

Pressure relief valve

Hinged rod

Exhaust shield

Liquid oxygen tank

Cork float valves

Pull cord

Alcohol burner

Oxygen gas pressure line

Gasoline tank

Pull cord

Oxygen cylinder

Check valve

Detachable starting hose

Pipe

Robert Goddard fired this liquid oxygen/gasoline rocket in 1926 at Auburn, Massachusetts. Within two and a half seconds, it reached a speed of 60 miles (96 km) per hour, soared 41 feet (12.5 m), and then crashed down 184 feet (56 m) from the launch site.

For the navy, Goddard developed a depth-charge rocket to use against the threat of submarines and a rocket that propelled armor-piercing warheads. By March 1923, the navy was finished with Goddard, and he began physical testing on his liquid-fueled engine designs. In 1924, he married Esther Christine Kisk, the daughter of Swedish immigrants.

Goddard's Kitty Hawk

Grants from various organizations trickled in over the next few years until finally, on March 16, 1926, the day Goddard had long been working toward came. After years of secretive labor, which included the issuing of numerous not-so-secret patents, the determined scientist successfully launched his first liquid-fueled rocket. Beginning back in 1916, some of Goddard's highly explosive experiments (many were failures) were conducted in Auburn, Massachusetts, on his aunt Effie Ward's ranch; therefore, it was in his aunt's cabbage patch that he launched this rocket. The 11-pound (5 kg) rocket was constructed from aluminum and magnesium alloy, stood within a frame 10 feet (3 m), and was built with the exhaust nozzle above the fuel tank. Goddard thought that his rocket would have a better flight if it were made to pull its own weight rather that push it.

Powered by gasoline and super-cooled liquid oxygen, the rocket flew 41 feet (12.5 m) into the air and crashed to the earth 184 feet (56 m) from the launch frame. The flight was not a perfect one, but the fact that it worked at all made Goddard ecstatic. For months afterward, he called his aunt's farm "his Kitty Hawk," comparing it to the North Carolina location where the Wright brothers conducted their first successful flight of a glider in 1900. In his usual style of secrecy, Goddard insisted that his financier, the Smithsonian Institution, keep his success a secret. Consequently, news about the first successful flight of a liquid-fueled rocket never reached the public.

By summer 1929, Goddard was back at his aunt's ranch in Auburn with a new liquid-fueled design that was another first in American history. The rocket weighed 57 pounds (26 kg), part of which was due to the addition of a camera, thermometer, and barometer. The camera was operated through a trip lever connected to the recovery parachute. In this sense, Goddard had developed America's first instrument-carrying rocket. Fame surrounding this successful launch, however, was not restricted to just this fact.

The blast from the 1929 rocket was so loud that it startled residents for miles around. The subsequent crash was even worse, as it caused a scorching grass fire in a hay field. People began fearing for their lives. Shortly afterward, the local fire marshal banned Goddard from further testing anywhere in the state of Massachusetts. Goddard received wide and unfavorable public attention as yet again the papers criticized the recent alarming antics of the "Moon Man."

Bad Press Brings Good News

The attention Goddard received from his 1929 launch, though all negative, drew the attention of world-renowned American aviator Charles Lindbergh (1902–74). Two years earlier, Lindbergh had become famous for conducting the first nonstop transatlantic solo flight between New York City and Paris in his monoplane, the *Spirit of St. Louis.* Lindbergh was an advocate for anything that had to do with new aviation technology and was immediately interested in helping further Goddard's research. He approached the Daniel Guggenheim Foundation to solicit rocket exploration funding on Goddard's behalf. Guggenheim pledged $100,000 toward Goddard's research but suggested he find more suitable surroundings in which to work.

In 1930, Goddard received two years' leave from Clark University and moved his headquarters to Roswell, New Mexico. He, his wife, and a crew of four trusted engineers set up home and shop on a 10-acre parcel called Mescalero Ranch. On a secluded plain 10 miles (6 km) away, Goddard constructed his launch tower. With plenty of money and no one around to interrupt him, Goddard set to work with a goal of designing bigger and better rockets.

While in Roswell, Goddard's secretiveness escalated to paranoid proportions as he made many advancements in his progressively larger rocket designs. In Europe at this time, Germany was testing its

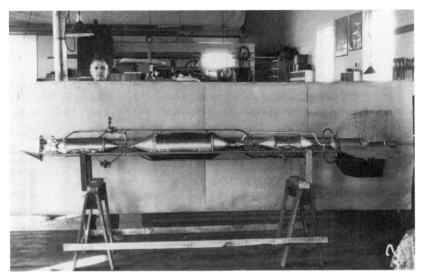

Goddard used this rocket in his first flight in Roswell, New Mexico, which took place on December 30, 1930. The rocket reached 2,000 feet (610 m), the highest flight achieved to that date. Goddard's machinist Henry Sachs is shown in the background. *(Photo courtesy of NASA)*

own rockets and rockets were all the rage, thanks in part to a 1923 book by Hermann Julius Oberth titled *Die rake zu den planetenräumen* (The rocket into planetary space). Goddard was not aware of Oberth's theories on rocketry; however, he was aware of the mounting world interest in being the first to build a high-altitude rocket and consequently was extremely protective of his designs. Later discoveries showed that some internal designs in Germany's famous V-2 rockets were suspiciously similar to Goddard's, though as years passed, the similarities were declared coincidental. Goddard, however, went to his grave believing otherwise.

On December 30, 1930, Goddard achieved his highest launch so far with his first flight in Roswell. His rocket attained an altitude of 2,000 feet (610 m) in seven seconds. Goddard recorded the event as a successful flight, though the typical instability continued to plague his rockets. Goddard realized there was an urgent need for a solution to keeping the rocket on course. What use was there for a rocket if it did not arrive at a desired destination?

Goddard soon completed a design for a gyroscopic stabilizer and integrated it into his rocket engine. When the rocket began to veer, theoretically the gyroscope would tip in the opposite direction, adjusting the vanes mounted near the exhaust and causing the rocket to tip back into the proper direction. By 1932, he launched his first rocket equipped with a gyroscopic stabilizer. The height achieved by this rocket was a disappointment, but the directional vanes worked, keeping the rocket on course! Goddard had just achieved a major advancement in rocket self-guidance.

The Reach for New Heights

From September 1934 to October 1935, Goddard occupied himself with perfecting his gyroscopic stabilizer. By July 1935, Goddard recorded success in his improved designs for gyroscopic control, engine concept, and blast vane steering mechanisms as his A-8 and A-10 rockets reached altitudes of more than a mile. Goddard launched 14 rockets in his "A" series.

In 1936, testing began on Goddard's larger "L" series rockets as he strove to achieve high-altitude flight. At first, they were slightly shorter that the "A" series, but at 18 inches around they had doubled in diameter. The problem with the professor's efforts in achieving extreme altitude was that he could not decide on which design process was best. The professor was a highly trained physicist, it was true, but he was not as talented at engineering, and his experiments were erratic. He of course had assistants, but they were limited in what they could offer.

In the "L" series, Goddard launched a total of 30 rockets, some with gyroscopes, some without, some with a large gaseous-nitrogen tank, some with a smaller liquid-nitrogen tank. Later designs grew to more than 18 feet and were slimmed back down to a nine-inch diameter. In 1937, Goddard's L-13 rocket achieved the highest altitude of all his rockets, reaching almost 9,000 feet (2,744 m), though a problem occurred with the parachute and it tore away without serving its purpose. The last rocket of the "L" series, L-30, was the most successful. Not in terms of height, as it achieved a reported 6,565 feet (2,000 m)—about 1,500 feet (457 m) short of L-13—but in terms of flawlessness. It soared into the sky in a beautifully vertical flight with a perfect deployment of the parachute.

A Broken Spirit

In an attempt to lighten the payload of his rockets and to discover a more efficient way to regulate the flow of fuels into the combustion chamber, in 1938 Goddard began making plans for an even

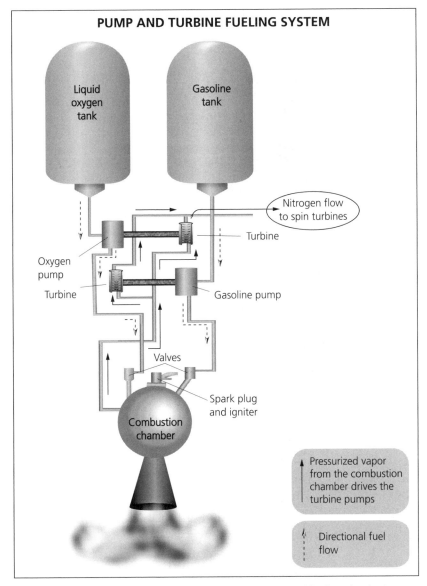

Simplified diagram of the pump and turbine fueling system Goddard used in his last series of rocket tests

One of Goddard's "P" series rockets as it waits in the launching tower at Roswell, New Mexico, on March 21, 1940

more efficient rocket engine. He designed a new lightweight, pump-turbine-driven unit that would potentially provide tremendous thrust through a self-sustained fuel-feeding system. These rockets, which he called the "P" series, resulted in the testing of 36 rockets. The "P" series would be his last attempt at reaching extreme heights.

The 24-foot (7.3-m) "P" series rocket was Goddard's most elaborate design, possessing all the best attributes of his knowledge of rocketry. Not only did it accommodate the newly designed pump-turbine engine, it was also equipped with a gyroscopic stabilizer, a high-pressure combustion chamber, lighter-weight fuel tanks, and, of course, a parachute deployment system.

Launch day for his first "P" series rocket came on February 9, 1940. Plenty of excitement surrounded the launch, but it turned out to be a disappointing failure when it blew apart at the launch tower. The cause was thought to be ice clogging the ignition. The second "P" rocket failed as well, as did all other "P" designs, one after another, for various reasons. The pump-turbine engine worked—that was not the problem. It was merely bad luck and wild mishaps keeping Goddard's flights from achieving success.

October 10, 1941, marked the end of experimentation for Goddard. The engine on rocket P-36 ignited, but this time the rocket jammed in the launch tower. The event was yet another failure. As the roiling flames died on the launch pad of P-36, so guttered the flame of Goddard's ambition. For years, his almost childlike enthusiasm kept his dreams of reaching space as dynamic as the day he descended from the cherry tree. Yet now, after so many torturous failures, Goddard's disappointment ran deep enough to turn the embers of hope into ashes of despair. His spirit finally broken, Goddard gave up on his lifelong dream of reaching extreme altitude. He never launched another rocket.

Goddard's Legacy

War once again loomed on America's horizon. Goddard offered his services to the U.S. Navy, and in September 1941, he began working under their contract to design a jet-assisted-take-off motor for aircraft, known as JATO. In July 1942, Goddard went to work full time in Annapolis, Maryland, at the Naval Engineering Experiment Station, where he remained until July 1945 supervising the development of the JATO.

Then, in June 1945, specialists diagnosed Goddard with throat cancer. Doctors conducted two surgeries, removing his trachea and his larynx. A cigar smoker all his life, Robert H. Goddard died on August 10, 1945, in a Baltimore, Maryland, hospital inside an oxygen tent.

Robert Goddard was responsible for almost single-handedly developing the modern rocket. His work did not attract the serious attention it deserved while he lived, which was partly his own fault. If not for his insistence on secrecy and his refusal of offers from the California Institute of Technology to provide Goddard with more talented engineers, the advancement of modern rocketry quite likely would have progressed at a much more rapid rate with a higher degree of success. Goddard was a physicist trying to do the job of an engineer without the proper training. It was not until the United States began a campaign to conquer space in the 1950s that Goddard's work began to be truly appreciated. Future designers soon discovered that building a rocket or launching a satellite without the designs patented by Goddard was impossible. To this day, his work remains a valuable part of any rocket design.

CHRONOLOGY

1882	Born on October 5 in Worcester, Massachusetts
1888–98	Begins school in Boston, attending Mount Pleasant, Hugh O'Brien, and English High

1898	Develops his first idea to build a device that could fly into space
1904	Enrolls at Worcester Polytechnic Institute
1908	Accepted to Clark University in Worcester
1911	Receives a doctorate in physics from Clark University
1912	accepted as a research fellow at Princeton University's Palmer Physical Laboratory; applies for his first patent for an oscillator
1914	Receives first two U.S. patents, for untested rocket propulsion designs; takes a part-time job as a physics instructor at Clark University
1915	First proves a rocket can operate in a vacuum
1919	Publishes his paper "A Method of Reaching Extreme Altitudes" through the Smithsonian Miscellaneous Collections
1920	Begins at Clark University as physics professor; begins designing weapons for the U.S. Navy
1923	Develops for the navy a depth-charge rocket and a rocket that propels armor-piercing warheads; begins physical testing on his liquid-fueled engine designs
1926	Launches the first successful liquid-fueled rocket on March 16
1929	Designs, builds, and (on July 17) launches America's first instrumented liquid-fueled rocket; draws the attention of Charles Lindbergh, who becomes an avid supporter
1930	Receives $100,000 in funding from the Daniel Guggenheim Foundation and moves his headquarters to Roswell, New Mexico
1932	Launches his first rocket designed with a gyroscopic stabilizer, instantly advancing the science of rocket guidance
1934	Begins his "A" series rocket tests in search of stability in flight

1936	Begins the "L" series of rocket tests in search of extreme altitude
1937	Rocket L-13 achieves the highest altitude of any of Goddard's rockets
1938	Begins designs on the "P" series rockets, all resulting in failure
1941	Finally gives up on building high-altitude rockets after his 36th attempt to fly a pump-turbine rocket. In September, he contracts to do jet-assisted-take-off (JATO) work for the U.S. Navy.
1942	Goes to work on JATO at the Naval Engineering Experiment Station in Annapolis, Maryland
1945	Dies from throat cancer on August 10 in Baltimore, Maryland

FURTHER READING

Books

Clary, David A. *Rocket Man: Robert H. Goddard and the Birth of the Space Age.* New York: Hyperion Press, 2003. A vivid portrayal of Robert Goddard's ingenious work. The author lends insight to Goddard's character along with well-researched data covering his scientific achievements.

Dewy, Anne Perkins. *Robert Goddard, Space Pioneer.* Boston: Little, Brown, 1962. A condensed history of Goddard's triumphs in rocketry with plenty of photos and illustrations.

Farley, Karin Clafford. *Robert H. Goddard (Pioneers in Change).* Englewood Cliffs, N.J.: Silver Burdett Press, 1991. A biography of Goddard and his pioneering efforts in the development of the first liquid fueled rocket. For ages 9–12.

Goddard, Robert H. *Rockets.* Reston, Va.: American Institute of Aeronautics and Astronautics, 2002. This book merges two significant publications by Robert Goddard, *A Method of Reaching Extreme Altitudes,* originally published in 1919, and *Liquid-Propellant Rocket Development,* originally published in 1936.

Lehman, Milton. *Robert H. Goddard: Pioneer of Space Research.* New York: Da Capo Press, 1963. A detailed account of Goddard's life achievements in rocketry that begins before the day of his birth and ends with the monuments of his success. Includes a few photographs and drawings.

Web Sites

Robert Hutchings Goddard Home Page. Available online. URL: http://www.clarku.edu/offices/library/archives/Goddard.htm. Accessed November 29, 2004. A Web site dedicated to Robert Goddard that includes more than a dozen pages, including drawings of his rockets and photos of his diary.

8

Wernher von Braun

(1912–1977)

Wernher von Braun was a key scientist in the development of rocketry in the 20th century and was an enthusiastic advocate for human exploration of space.

The Twentieth Century's Foremost Rocket Engineer

The German physicist Wernher von Braun was one of the most important rocket scientists and champions of space exploration from the 1930s to the 1970s. He is well known as being the developer of the famous V-2 missile built by Nazi Germany during World War II. After the war, having become a U.S. citizen, he became director of the U.S. Marshall Space Flight Center in Huntsville, Alabama, affiliated with the National Aeronautics and

Space Administration (NASA), and became famous for leading the research and design of the superbooster *Saturn V* launch vehicle, which carried the first American *astronauts* to the Moon.

Aristocratic Heritage

Wernher von Braun was born Wernher Magnus Maximilian Freiherr von Braun in Wirsitz, in East Prussia (now Wyrzysk, Poland) on March 23, 1912. He was the second of three sons born to Baron Magnus von Braun, who served as secretary of agriculture during the Nazi regime, and Baroness Emmy von Quistorp.

Wernher was born during a period of unrest in his country. By the time he was two, World War I broke out. It did not end until Germany's defeat in 1918. In an attempt to rebuild their country, Germans did away with the traditional autocratic form of rule in favor of a democracy known as the Weimar Republic. When Wirsitz was given to Poland in 1920, the von Brauns moved to Berlin. At this time, Berlin was known as a gathering place for famous scientific greats such as Albert Einstein (1879–1955), Max Planck (1858–1947), and Erwin Schrödinger (1887–1961), who would assemble for lectures and to share knowledge.

It was in this environment of scientific and social revolution that young Wernher began his education. Excitement in rocket technology was at a new height. Wernher and his older brother Sigismund would purchase fireworks and ignite them with great enthusiasm. Sigismund eventually tired of the fireworks, but Wernher did not. Rockets and their potential fascinated him. At age 13, he attached a cluster of fireworks to the back of a wagon and sent it careening down the avenue, where it burst to flames, resulting in his arrest.

In the early years of his education, Wernher was what some might have called a daydreamer. He did well in music and art, but scored poorly in subjects such as math and physics, not for lack of reasoning power, but for lack of interest. Then, on the day of his Catholic confirmation, his mother presented him with a telescope. Wernher spent hours with the telescope, peering at the night sky and letting his imagination run away with him. This began a love affair with space that helped interest him in physics.

A Man with a Singular Vision

After receiving the telescope, Wernher gained an interest in science fiction that would influence the entire course of his future. He read the novels of space travel visionaries, such as Jules Verne's *From the Earth to the Moon* and H. G. Wells's *War of the Worlds*. The book that had the most profound effect on him was one by German space travel theorist Hermann Julius Oberth, titled *Die rake zu den planetenräumen* (The rocket into planetary space, 1923). In 1925, after reading Oberth's theory on piloted space flight, which included a diagram of a rocket, a single grand idea suddenly grasped Wernher's mind. It was an idea that would drive all his future decisions. He would build a rocket, one that would carry humankind into space. Toward this goal, Wernher knew he first needed to accomplish one important thing: an unerring understanding of physics.

In 1928, Baron von Braun enrolled his son in a boarding school, the Hermann Lietz School, in ancient Ettersburg Castle, near Weimar in central Germany. At Ettersburg, the educational curriculum included not only academics but also the development of technical skills such as carpentry and bricklaying. During the day, the school kept Wernher's active mind busy, and in the evenings he was allowed one or two hours with his small telescope.

In 1930, von Braun entered the Berlin Institute of Technology (BIT). There, he earned a bachelor's degree in mechanical engineering in 1932. While attending BIT, von Braun became a member of the newly formed amateur rocket building society known as the VfR (Verein für Raumschiffahrt, or Society for Space Travel).

Von Braun's participation in the VfR was as ambitious as any of the founding members, including fellow member Hermann Oberth, von Braun's first true source of inspiration. Oberth and von Braun quickly became friends. In 1930, the VfR relocated to Raketenflugplatz, the abandoned military dump outside Berlin. Between 1930 and 1931, the VfR succeeded in launching 87 test rockets with engines of various design. They also conducted 270 static tests, in which the rocket engine is test-fired and does not leaving the ground.

The idea of putting a person into space was the single great idea in von Braun's mind. Yet there were many questions regarding

The VfR (Verein für Raumschiffahrt, or Society for Space Travel)

Willy Ley (1906–69), Max Valier (1895–1930), and Johannes Winkler (1897–1947) founded this society on July 5, 1927, in Breslau, Germany. The goal of the VfR was to raise funds to finance the rocket experiments of space travel visionaries such as their countryman Hermann Oberth (1894–1989). The official charter set forth for the society outlined two goals: to popularize the idea of rocket flight to the Moon and outer planets and to conduct serious experiments in rocket propulsion development.

By 1929, the VfR had 870 members. Later, it grew to 1,000. Though funding was usually tight, by 1930 the society had succeeded in launching the first rocket car, in Rüsselsheim, Germany, driven by Kurt Volkhart, and a rocket glider at Rebstock, near Frankfurt, flown by Fritz von Opel. The club also acquired an old military dump outside Berlin that they called Raketenflugplatz (rocket airfield), which they used for testing their rockets.

By 1932, the rockets of the VfR had a range of about three miles (5 km) and could reach an altitude of about 5,000 feet (1,525 m), though the results were always inconsistent and the rockets were plagued with instability and overheating. In this same year, the German army became interested in liquid-fueled rockets and took notice of the work being done by the VfR, taking a special interest in one particularly enthusiastic member, Wernher von Braun. By 1933, Adolf Hitler came into power and the VfR collapsed for reasons of financial turmoil and restrictions on private experimentation in rocketry imposed by the Nazi regime. The remaining members of the VfR were absorbed into the Fortschrittliche Verkehrstechnik, E.V. (EVFV—Society for Progress in Traffic Techniques).

space travel, such as how would a body react in space? To help answer this question, in 1931 he and a medical student named Constantine Generales built out of a bicycle wheel a crude centrifuge that utilized white mice as test subjects. The device was designed to reproduce the effects of acceleration on a body, such as the force one would experience in a rocket traveling fast enough to breach the gravitational pull of the Earth. The results of the experiments were not favorable for the mice and showed that for humans to achieve piloted space flight, measures would need to be taken to safeguard against the effects of *g force*.

Opportunity Knocks

In 1932, the VfR prepared a liquid-fueled rocket demonstration for an audience of military personnel at their Raketenflugplatz launch site. Their experiments were beset with the usual problems of instability and overheating, and the demonstration was less than a success. Von Braun, however, made an impression on Captain Walter Dornberger of the German army. Dornberger presented von Braun to his boss, Colonel Karl Becker, who offered von Braun a civilian position developing rockets for the army under the condition that he earn his doctorate in physics at the University of Berlin. To the young scientist, this was a huge break. Von Braun accepted the position, though he knew he would be asked to develop ballistic weapons. He nevertheless saw it as an opportunity to further his idealistic goal of someday sending humans into space in a liquid-fueled rocket.

On October 1, 1932, Wernher von Braun became a civilian employee of the German army. In 1933, he moved to the army installation at Kummersdorf, 20 miles (32 km) south of Berlin, where the army supplied him with a test station and three colleagues. He entered the University of Berlin, and in 1934 he earned a doctorate in physics with a thesis on liquid rocket propulsion.

At Kummersdorf, von Braun and his team worked on the same problems he experienced while with the VfR, including the big problem of the lack of rocket guidance. The team was soon ready to launch its first liquid-fueled rocket, named the *Aggregat 1*, or *A-1*, which employed a finless guidance system based solely on a gyroscopic spinner placed in the nose cone. The rocket was 55 inches (140 cm) in length and weighed 85 pounds (39 kg). Its fuel was alcohol and liquid oxygen, with pressurized nitrogen in a separate tank used to force the propellants into the combustion chamber. The gyroscopic guidance system in the nose proved inadequate, rendering the flight a failure.

Replacing the *A-1* design was the *A-2*, which repositioned the gyroscopic spinner to the middle of the rocket in an attempt to make the device less top-heavy. This design worked, with the rocket reaching an altitude of 6,500 feet (1981 m) by the end of 1934. At this time, von Braun's *A-2* rocket was superior to all previous rocket technology.

While von Braun was busy testing rockets, Adolf Hitler, director of the Nazi (National Socialist) Party, had become the new chancellor of Germany. The new Nazi regime prohibited rocket testing to all except the government, which caused the dissolution of the VfR. It was during this time that the German air force, called the Luftwaffe, became interested in rocket power as a supplement to its propeller-driven aircraft, to provide short bursts of power and speed. Upon being asked, von Braun set to work on designing a rocket for this purpose.

By this time, von Braun had earned his pilot's license. In 1936, the Kummersdorf team, with von Braun at the controls, successfully proved that rocket power could work on regular aircraft. Between 1936 and 1938, he served in the Luftwaffe and qualified to fly fighter planes, such as the Messerschmidtt, and dive bombers, such as the Stuka.

Joint Forces

In 1936, the German army and the Luftwaffe teamed together to form a new military rocket base near the village of Peenemünde, on the northwestern shores of the Baltic Sea 150 miles (241 km) north of Berlin. In 1937, von Braun moved most of his team to the partially completed facility and became the technical director for the army's rocket testing program. He and his team began design on what would become the world's first long-range ballistic missile. The base was completed in 1939.

Von Braun's team conducted many tests on improving rocket guidance systems, which included dropping test vehicles from bombers at 20,000 feet and filming their behavior as they plummeted to the Earth while reaching supersonic speeds.

On October 3, 1942, the Peenemünde team launched the highly anticipated *A-4*. The 12-ton (11,000 kg) rocket flew 60 miles (96 km) high and 120 miles (192 km) downrange, landing 1.5 miles (2.4 km) from its intended target. The flight was a complete success, and the *A-4* became the world's first guided ballistic missile, breaking the world altitude record of 24 miles (40 km) formerly held by the Paris Gun, a ballistic shell designed by the German navy and first used to shell Paris in 1918.

The Wrong Planet

With the success of the *A-4*, Hitler decided to use von Braun's rocket as a propaganda weapon and ordered it into production. This was not a small task, and the work went slowly. Shortages of materials

This upward shot of the twin engines of *Titan I* rocket shows just a small example of the complexity involved in a fully assembled rocket engine. The photo inset is taken of the same rocket engines from a distance. *(Photo by Scott McCutcheon)*

A *V-2* rocket launches from a site at White Sands, New Mexico, in 1946 after von Braun and his team began making rockets for the United States. *(Photo courtesy of NASA)*

along with technical and financial delays impeded progress. To put the magnitude of a successfully built rocket into perspective, each rocket had 90,000 parts and was individually hand-crafted. Hitler wanted this complex device ready for mass production and he was growing impatient.

More than 60,000 design changes took place on the rocket until the final device was realized. It stood 46 feet (14 m) high, was 5.5 feet (1.7 m) wide and weighed 28,000 pounds (13,000 kg). On September 8, 1944, the *A-4*— renamed the *V-2* (*Vergeltungswaffe 2*, or Vengeance Weapon 2)— was launched from a mobile launch platform and the first guided-missile-delivered warhead fell on England, Germany's enemy.

This was the largest and most complex rocket ever built up until that time, and it was just the beginning. A new slave labor camp in the Harz Mountains called Mittelwerk (Central Works) was soon turning out *V-2s* on an assembly line, producing more than 600 rockets per month. By the time the war ended, Germany had produced nearly 6,000 bomb-packing *V-2s*, with more than 3,000 of those landing in England, France, Belgium, and the Netherlands, causing the deaths of thousands of people. Despite the apparent military success of the *V-2*, it did not turn the tide of war as Hitler had hoped, and his reign of terror ended in defeat. Fortunately, von Braun's dream of launching a rocket into space did not die.

From Adversary to Ally

By spring 1945, World War II came to an end. The Allied forces won after pushing the front line back beyond the 180-mile (290-km) range of the *V-2*. Hitler committed suicide. Von Braun and his

Peenemünde crew surrendered under friendly terms to the Americans. In September 1945, von Braun and his hand-picked team of rocket scientists arrived at an army installation at Fort Bliss, Texas, where they began a life carefully structured, isolated, and controlled by the U.S. government. Their job, called the Hermes project, was to assemble and test the 793,000 pounds (360,000 kg) of *V-2* rocket parts captured and shipped in from Germany. The living conditions were similar to those of prisoners on work release. Pay was low and so was morale. Von Braun convinced his associates to continue their work and to do their best because, bad as the future might look then, this was still an ongoing opportunity to try and build a rocket that would travel into space.

Between 1945 and 1950, von Braun's team fired the *V-2s* from the White Sands Proving Ground in New Mexico, a testing complex developed in 1945 for the exclusive purpose of advancing the technology of rocketry. The second rocket launched from White Sands in May 1946 carried in its ample payload compartment, not explosives, but instrumentation to better understand the atmosphere. On that day, the world's first high-altitude rocket began the world's first exploration of space. In October, the first motion-picture camera to be launched aboard a *V-2* returned the first black-and-white film of the curvature of the Earth against the black background of space. It was a triumphant moment for science. Ironically, Hitler's device of terror and destruction was now transformed into an instrument of curiosity that could further the growth of space exploration.

The Space Race

In 1947, von Braun briefly returned to Germany to marry Maria Louise von Quinstorp, his cousin. Then, in 1950, he and his new family moved to Huntsville, Alabama, along with his team of scientists. They went to work there for the Army Ballistic Missile Agency at Redstone Arsenal. At Redstone, Von Braun worked on the *Redstone*, *Jupiter*, and *Jupiter-C* rockets. In 1952, von Braun published his first book, titled *The Mars Project*, initially through a German publisher and then in 1953 through an American publisher. In *The Mars Project*, he outlined his plans for space travel and planetary exploration.

The United States, however, was not the only nation developing rockets. Despite all the efforts of the U.S. government to be the first to send a satellite into space, on October 4, 1957, the Union of Soviet Socialist Republics (USSR) *R-7* rocket, developed by Sergei Korolyov (1907–66), carried a 184-pound (83-kg) satellite the size of a basketball into orbit. The name of this historic satellite is *Sputnik.* The news that the Soviets preceded the United States into space was devastating, and the worst was yet to come. One month later, the USSR launched a second *R-7* carrying *Sputnik 2,* a huge satellite weighing 1,120 pounds (508 kg), along with a dog named Laika, which survived for only one day because of *capsule* overheating. The damage was done. The Soviets became the first to prove they could put a living being into orbit, though they had not yet developed a way to bring it back.

The U.S. response to the Soviet success was a dismal failure. Instead of going with von Braun's tried and tested *Redstone* rocket, President Eisenhower chose to go with a navy-developed rocket called the *Vanguard,* which had never been developed beyond the drawing board. Von Braun was deeply frustrated, claiming the navy rocket was untested and therefore invited failure. His team, he said, could have had the satellite in space within 60 days. True to von Braun's doubts, the *Vanguard,* carrying a tiny four-pound (1.81 kg) satellite, exploded on the launch pad.

Naturally, the next attempt went to the Redstone team, and on January 31, 1958, von Braun's *Jupiter-C* rocket carried *Explorer 1,* the first U.S. satellite, into orbit. In the same year, the missions of *Pioneers 1–3* failed to bring back photos of the Moon, yet they succeeded in providing new information on the area between the Earth and the Moon, including data on the Van Allen radiation belts. Then on March 3, 1959, von Braun's team launched the *Pioneer 4* Moon probe, which missed the Moon but became the first spacecraft to orbit the Sun. In 1960, *Pioneer 5* studied space between Venus and the Earth.

Despite the success of *Explorer 1* and the partial successes of early *Pioneer* probes, the rocket technology of the United States was still inferior to Soviet rocket technology. The race for space was in full motion.

In 1958, President Eisenhower established the National Aeronautics and Space Administration (NASA), and talks began on how to proceed with a piloted lunar landing conducted by the United States. Toward this goal, the George C. Marshall Space Flight Center was established in Huntsville, Alabama, next door to the Redstone Arsenal. In 1960, von Braun was appointed as its first director. He and his team quit work for the army and began work for NASA, moving their operations to the nearby Marshall Space Flight Center.

The Pressure Mounts

On April 12, 1961, to the consternation of the United States, the USSR announced the successful placement of the first man in space. Cosmonaut Yuri Alexeyevich Gagarin (1934–68) successfully orbited the Earth one time aboard the *Vostok 1* for an astonishing one hour and 48 minutes at an altitude of 187 miles (302 kilometers) and a speed of 18,000 miles (28,962 km) an hour. The next month, on May 5, the United States succeeded in sending astronaut Alan Shepard into the upper atmosphere aboard one of von Braun's modified *Redstone* rockets. Shepard became the first American in space, though his 15-minute flight—which never achieved Earth orbit— paled in comparison to the flight of the *Vostok 1*.

On May 25, 1961, an announcement came from President John F. Kennedy declaring that winning the space race was a national priority. One historic sentence stood out:

"I believe that this nation should commit itself to achieving the goal before this decade is out of landing a man on the Moon and returning him safely to Earth."

Those few words from President Kennedy generated $25 billion toward rocket research and made possible von Braun's vision of space travel and planetary exploration. Soon afterward, the Apollo space program was born. Included in the U.S. race for space was the Mercury program, established in 1958 with the goal of placing a man in orbit and returning him to Earth. Also included was the Gemini program, established in 1961 with the goal of exploring and developing humankind's capabilities to work in the environment of space.

Now the challenge was great. Landing the first man on the Moon was much different from the previous goal of merely a circumlunar mission, which did not involve a landing. While the Space Task Force team at Langley Research Center in Virginia was responsible for designing the capsule in which the astronauts would ride, it was von Braun and his team's responsibility to create a rocket powerful enough to propel the payload of a lunar lander and all that it necessitated into outer space. The U.S. Air Force had its *Atlas* rocket (which made it possible for astronaut John Glenn to become the first American to completely orbit the Earth on February 20, 1962), but the *Atlas* was not capable of enough thrust to escape Earth's gravity while pushing a fully loaded *command module* and a *lunar module*. The *Saturn* series rocket, or superbooster, was chosen for this task. Von Braun became the chief architect of what would become the *Saturn V* launch vehicle, the most massive rocket design ever imagined.

From Out of the Blue

The first *Saturn* rocket, *S-1*, was launched unpiloted from Cape Canaveral in Florida, on October 27, 1961. (Cape Canaveral was later renamed the John F. Kennedy Space Center in December 1963.) The *Saturn S-1* was 162 feet (49 m) tall and weighed 460 tons (471,000 kg) when fully loaded with its payload of water. It supported a cluster of eight engines, nicknamed "Cluster's Last Stand." The outer four were gimbaled for guidance. The rocket generated 1.5 million pounds (6,700 kn) of thrust. Intended to verify the structure and *aerodynamics* of the vehicle, the launch was a complete success. During its eight-minute flight, *S-1* reached an altitude of 85 miles (137 km), splashing down in the Atlantic Ocean 214 miles (344 km) downrange. Out from the blue sky and into the blackness of space, humankind extended its first tendril of cutting-edge technology toward planetary exploration. The *Saturn* design concept was approved; however, it was soon realized that greater power was needed. Engines capable of 1.5 million pounds (6,700 kn) of thrust each would be necessary to place a man on the Moon.

Von Braun and his team began work on the *Saturn V*, a gigantic three-stage version of the original *S-1*. The first stage consisted of a cluster of five engines called *F-1* engines, the largest liquid-fuel rocket engines ever designed. The *F-1* contained a high-speed fuel pump capable of delivering liquid oxygen and kerosene fuel at an astonishing rate of three tons (2.7 mt) per second. Cumulatively, this first stage yielded more than 7.5 million pounds (33,500 kn) of thrust. Generating more than 200,000 pounds (890 kn) of thrust each, the new *J-2* engine powered the two upper stages, burning highly volatile liquid hydrogen, which required a storage temperature of –423° Fahrenheit (–253° C). In terms of mission success, it was the unsurpassed power and efficiency of the extremely cold liquid hydrogen that made it possible to launch a man to the Moon. The final design of the *Saturn V* was 281 feet (86 m) tall and 33 feet (10 m) in diameter, with the *Apollo* command module adding another 82 feet (25 m) to the top. It was a far greater beast than the rockets von Braun had first developed back at Kummersdorf and greater still than the first liquid-fueled device fired by American physicist Robert Goddard (1882–1945) back in 1926, which stood only 10 feet (3 m) tall.

The first test launch for the *Saturn V* occurred on November 9, 1967, and the roar of the engines rose to an earsplitting 120 decibels. There was no question as to whether the rocket lifted off, but whether Florida had sunk. The flight and its stages were a complete success, as was the recovery of the *service module* after it reentered Earth's atmosphere and splashed down intact, 26 miles (42 km) from the target landing zone.

The Pinnacle of Success

The first flight carrying astronauts happened with *Apollo 7*, which launched from a *Saturn 1B* rocket on October 11, 1968. Aboard was Commander Walter M. Schirra, command module pilot Donn F. Eisele, and lunar module pilot R. Walter Cunningham. The flight lasted 10 days, 20 hours, and made 163 orbits of the Earth. The first flight aimed toward the Moon happened with *Apollo 8*, which launched on December 21, 1968, from a thundering *Saturn V* rocket. Aboard was Commander Frank Borman, command module pilot James A. Lovell, and lunar module pilot William A. Anders. The spacecraft entered lunar orbit on Christmas Eve, December 24, 1968, and became the first piloted space flight to orbit the Moon and the first to send back pictures of the lunar surface and a view of the

Apollo 11, aboard a *Saturn V* superbooster rocket, lifts off from the Kennedy Space Center on December 16, 1969, on the first piloted mission to land on the Moon. *(Photo Courtesy of NASA)*

Earth from space. The piloted flights of *Apollo 9* and *Apollo 10* followed, until NASA was finally ready to send a lander to the Moon. On July 16, 1969, *Apollo 11* lifted off under a *Saturn V* rocket carrying Commander Neil A. Armstrong, command module pilot Michael Collins, and lunar module pilot Edwin E. (Buzz) Aldrin.

The rocket lifted off from the Kennedy Space Flight Center while von Braun and the rest of the launch officials observed from the launch control center three miles away. For von Braun, this was the pinnacle of more than 45 years of work. His dream was a now a reality. Humanity was on its way to the Moon! Four days later, the famous words spoken by Commander Neil Armstrong came over the intercom at mission control in Houston: "Houston, Tranquility Base here . . . the Eagle has landed."

Seven hours after that, Armstrong became the first man to set foot on a planetary body other than the Earth. Von Braun was a key individual among the hundreds of talented personnel that worked together to make that day happen. It was the height of von Braun's career.

A Visionary to the End

In 1970, after the end of the Apollo program, von Braun moved with his family from their longtime home in Huntsville to Washington, D.C., where he served as deputy associate administrator for strategic planning at NASA headquarters. He made this decision after realizing that the Nixon administration and the United States no longer shared his enthusiasm and visions for a mission to Mars.

Von Braun stayed with NASA for two more years, but the excitement that carried the space program through the 1960s did not pass over into 1970s. In 1972, he retired from NASA and became the vice-president of engineering and development for Fairchild Industries, a private *aerospace* engineering company in Germantown, Maryland.

Even after achieving his dream of putting a man on the Moon, von Braun continued to campaign for the exploration of space. In 1973, he was inducted into the U.S. Army Ordnance Corps Hall of Fame, which was established on May 9, 1969, to recognize individuals who have made a positive and significant contribution to the U.S. Army Ordnance Corps. In 1974, he founded the National Space Institute, now called the National Space Society, whose goal is to advance the day when people will live and work in space. He continued to remain in the public eye, appearing at launchings at the Kennedy Space Center and speaking elatedly in front of the camera about space exploration. In 1977, as he lay ill in his hospital bed, the chairman of Fairchild Industries, Edward G. Uhl, presented him with the National Medal of Science, awarded to von Braun by President Gerald R. Ford. A few years after joining Fairchild, von Braun learned he had cancer. He underwent surgery, but the procedure was not a success. His health began to fail, and on December 31, 1976, he retired from Fairchild. On June 16, 1977, Wernher von Braun died in Alexandria, Virginia, at age 65.

Under the direction of Wernher von Braun came the world's most powerful rockets and the realization of the first exploration of space by man and machine. The creation of the *Saturn* rocket series enabled *Skylab*, the world's first occupied space station, to launch for orbit on May 14, 1973, which was also the last day a *Saturn* rocket would ever tear through the sky of the Earth. Throughout his life, von Braun received numerous awards for his contributions to science and to the U.S. space effort in particular. He was a member of several science societies, the author of several books and articles, and held honorary doctorate degrees from many universities and colleges. On the day of his death, he was remembered by a nation and in the words of President Jimmy Carter:

> To millions of Americans, Wernher von Braun's name was inextricably linked to our exploration of space and to the creative application of technology. . . . Not just the people of our nation, but all the people of the world have profited from his work.

CHRONOLOGY

1912	Born on March 23 in Wirsitz, Prussia (now Wyrzysk, Poland)
1928	Enrolls in a boarding school at Ettersburg Castle and becomes interested in rocketry and space flight
1930	Enters the Berlin Institute of Technology, where he begins experimenting with liquid-fueled rocket engines; becomes a member of a private German rocket society called the VfR (Verein für Raumschiffahrt, or Society for Space Travel)
1931	Builds a centrifuge to test the effects of acceleration (g force) on test mice
1932	Earns a bachelor's degree in mechanical engineering from the Berlin Institute of Technology; is employed by the German army to develop rockets

1933	Moves to the army installation at Kummersdorf to research rocket propulsion; becomes a licensed pilot
1934	Earns a doctorate in physics from the University of Berlin and launches his first successful Kummersdorf rocket called the *A-2*
1936–38	Proves that jet-assisted take-off (JATO) could work on human-powered aircraft; serves part time in the Luftwaffe
1937	Moves with his team to the military base at Peenemünde, where he becomes technical director for the German army's rocket testing program
1942	The *A-4* launches successfully and becomes the world's first piloted missile
1944	On September 8, the *A-4*, renamed the *V-2*, is launched on England and becomes the first guided missile to carry a warhead
1945–50	Surrenders (with his colleagues) to the Americans as World War II ends; the team will spend five years assembling and testing the remaining captured *V-2* rockets at White Sands Proving Ground in New Mexico.
1946	In October the first rocket carrying a motion picture camera is launched from White Sands Proving Ground and returns the first film of the curvature of the Earth
1947	Marries his cousin Maria Louise von Quinstorp on March 1, in Bavaria
1950	Moves to Huntsville, Alabama, to work for the Army Ballistic Missile Agency at Redstone Arsenal
1952	Publishes his first book, *The Mars Project,* through a German publisher, in which he outlines his plans for space travel and planetary exploration
1955	Becomes a U.S. citizen
1958	*Jupiter-C* rocket carries *Explorer 1,* the first U.S. satellite, into orbit. President Eisenhower establishes the National

	Aeronautics and Space Administration (NASA) in Huntsville, Alabama.
1960	Becomes first director of NASA's newly built Marshall Space Flight Center and is put in charge of designing the *Saturn V* launch vehicle, intended to carry humans to the Moon
1961	The first *Saturn* test rocket, *S-1,* is launched unpiloted from Cape Canaveral in Florida
1967	The first test launch of the gigantic *Saturn V* superbooster
1968	*Apollo 7/Saturn 1B* spacecraft becomes the first flight carrying U.S. astronauts into space. *Apollo 8/Saturn V* becomes the first piloted flight to orbit the Moon.
1969	*Apollo 11/Saturn V* spacecraft successfully carries out the first mission to land a person on the Moon
1970	Moves to Washington, D.C., to serve as deputy associate administrator of NASA headquarters
1972	Retires from NASA and becomes the vice president of engineering and development for Fairchild Industries in Germantown, Maryland
1973	*Saturn V/Skylab* is launched; no *Saturn V* rocket has been built since
1974	Founds the National Space Society, which today is widely known as the foremost citizen's voice on space
1976	Retires after learning he has cancer
1977	Dies on June 16 in Alexandria, Virginia

FURTHER READING
Books

Ordway, Frederick I., III, and Mitchell R. Sharp. *The Rocket Team.* Burlington, Ontario: Apogee Books, 2003. A complete history of the team behind Germany's *V-2* rocket program, of which

Wernher von Braun was the leader. Includes a DVD of rare footage of 1920s German rocket pioneers in action.

Spangenburg, Ray, and Diane K. Moser. *Wernher Von Braun: Space Visionary and Rocket Engineer.* New York: Facts On File, 1995. A good overview of the life and achievements of Wernher von Braun. Intended as an accessible biography for the layperson.

Von Braun, Wernher, and Frederick I. Ordway III. *The Rockets' Red Glare.* New York: Anchor Press/Doubleday. A history of rocketry from antiquity to modern times, written by two of the world's foremost authorities on rockets. Includes photos and lithographs.

Ward, Bob, and John Glenn. *Mr. Space: The Life of Wernher von Braun.* Washington, D.C.: Smithsonian Institution Press, 2004. Ten years in the making, this is a well-researched, authoritative biography of Wernher von Braun. Includes 50 photographs.

Winter, Frank H. *Prelude to the Space Age: The Rocket Societies, 1924–1940.* Washington, D.C.: Smithsonian Institution Press, 1983. A thorough account of the early dreams of rocketry and the different societies that formed to carry out what became significant rocket research.

Web Sites

"The Apollo Program." Smithsonian National Air and Space Museum. Available online. URL: http://www.nasm.si.edu/collections/imagery/apollo/apollolaunches.htm. Accessed November 29, 2004. A chronological list of all the Apollo missions from 1966 through 1975. Includes information on each mission, such as the launch vehicle used, the date of the launch, and the mission parameters and milestone accomplishments.

"Von Braun Astronomical Society." Available online. URL: http://www.vbas.org. Accessed November 29, 2004. Located in Monte Sano State Park, near Huntsville, Alabama, the Von Braun Astronomical Society is a nonprofit volunteer organization of amateur and professional astronomers who operate a planetarium and observatory. The Web site offers news, an ephemeris, a listing of projects, links to other sites, and information on becoming a member.

9

Carl Sagan

(1934–1996)

Carl Sagan is known for popularizing space science to the general public and for his scientific approach to attempting to discover life on other worlds. *(Photo courtesy of AIP Emilio Segrè Visual Archives, John Irwin Collection)*

Modern Popularizer of Space Science and Cofounder of the New Field of Exobiology

The American astronomer Carl E. Sagan is deemed the world's most famous popularizer of science, in particular the disciplines of astronomy and the search for life beyond Earth. As a passionate and modern freethinker, he was the first to ignore the open criticism of his professional peers and introduce the search for extraterrestrial life as a serious scientific subject, and was subsequently responsible for placing numerous life-searching scientific experiments on unpiloted space probes. Using a rising new technological phenomenon called the electronic media, otherwise known as television, Carl Sagan established a global campaign toward the public education of science and brought about a nationwide understanding of astronomy like no other astronomer before him.

Born in Brooklyn

Carl Edward Sagan was born during the height of the Great Depression on November 9, 1934, in Bensonhurst, a section of Brooklyn, New York. His father, Samuel Sagan, was born in Russia, immigrated to America when he was five, and as an adult worked in an apparel factory. His mother, Rachel, was an American-born woman of European descent. While Carl was growing up, little did anyone realize that this typical American boy would someday become the world's most popular astronomer of his time.

In 1939, when Carl was five years old, his family took him to the New York World's Fair. The fair's futuristic theme made an instant and lasting impression on him. It changed the way he thought about the subject of science and gave rise to the beginning of a passionate and everlasting fascination with stars and planets.

When he was about eight years old, Carl picked up a book by Edgar Rice Burroughs called *A Princess of Mars* (1912), about a hero who somehow teleported himself to Mars, where he found an entirely new civilization. Carl wanted to believe in Burroughs's Martian civilization, but by age nine he began to question Burroughs's application of science, or rather the complete lack of it. Carl was very intelligent and he longed for proof. In his young mind, the idea of life existing someplace other than Earth suddenly took shape. This idea helped to spark the flame that would kindle into a lifelong quest: the scientific search for extraterrestrial life.

How Will You Make a Living?

According to William Poundstone's *Carl Sagan: A Life in the Cosmos*, when Carl revealed to his family that he wanted to become an astronomer, his grandfather quickly replied, "Yes, but how will you make a living?" To the average person in the 1940s, astronomy was very obscure. Outside of scientific circles, few people knew much about it and therefore making a living by studying astronomy seemed absurd. Carl's hopes crashed as he began to see himself in some dreary office job with only a few hours at night during which to stargaze.

In 1948, his father received a promotion to manage a new coat factory in Perth Amboy, New Jersey. By this time, Carl's teachers had recognized he was gifted and suggested he attend a private school. Instead, his parents elected to keep him in the public school system, though he was promoted a couple of grades ahead. Soon after the move to New Jersey, he began to attend Rahway High School, a waste of time, according to Carl, at least where science class was concerned.

Then one day during his sophomore year, his biology teacher informed him that despite what his grandfather had said, it was quite possible for a person to make a living as an astronomer. That was all Carl needed to hear. Under the shadow of his parents' silent frowns, he learned the names of and sent out letters to various astronomers. Carl was determined to do with his life what he wanted and not become the concert pianist his mother dreamed of or to follow in the footsteps of his father through the doors of the coat factory. To his joy, some of the astronomers sent favorable replies, reinforcing the fact that astronomy did indeed exist as a profession.

The American Dream

Bent on a future as an astronomer, Sagan enrolled in the University of Chicago in 1951, due to its academic prestige and because it was one of the few universities that would accept him at age 17. The school also employed some of the country's finest science educators. If there was one thing about living in America that was understood throughout much of the world, it was having the opportunity to do with one's life what one wanted. This pursuit of happiness is known as the American dream. Sagan was about to embark on his own American dream.

The next few years saw many changes in Sagan's busy life. He studied, played basketball (he stood six foot one), cofounded astronomy and science fiction clubs, and conquered the summits of his education. His interests were boundless, and he worked in areas of astronomy, cosmology, biology, and the philosophy of science. Yet his greatest interest lay in life's origins and the possibility of its existence outside of Earth. While attending the university, Sagan made some of his best social contacts and began making a name for himself. He was competitive, intelligent, and hardworking, traits that impressed many people.

A New Field of Science

Sagan, though an idealist, was always interested in the facts behind the fantasies, and his intelligence earned him the respect and friendship of the American geneticist Hermann Muller, who in 1946 received the Nobel Prize in physiology for the discovery of the production of mutations by means of X-ray irradiation. Sagan spent the summers of 1952 and 1953 working in Muller's lab, raising and sorting (by gender) fruit flies for Muller's experiments. He spent many hours discussing the possibility of extraterrestrial life with Muller. In W. Poundstone's *A Life in the Cosmos*, Sagan stated that, "If not for meeting Muller, I might possibly have bowed under the weight of conventional opinion that all these subjects (on extraterrestrials) were nonsense."

Muller introduced Sagan to American chemist and Nobel laureate Harold Clayton Urey and also, eventually, to Stuart Miller, one of his graduate students. Urey, who in 1934 won the Nobel Prize in chemistry for his discovery of heavy hydrogen, had a deep interest in the chemistry of planets and how they might relate to the origins of life. His studies brought about the Miller-Urey experiment, which simulated conditions as they may have been during prehistoric Earth when the processes that began life were first coming together. Sagan was one of very few scientists who grasped the significance of the experiment's results, which showed that the elements required to fos-

The Dark Bands of Mars

NASA's *Mariner 4*, which launched on November 28, 1964, was the first spacecraft to obtain and transmit close-range images of Mars. Contrary to the popular belief at the time that the dark bands across the surface were evidence of botanical life, the relayed surface images from *Mariner 4* revealed a dry, cratered, moonlike surface where no evidence of plant life existed. This did not answer the question as to what the dark bands were, but more as to what the dark bands were not.

Today, it is known that the dark bands on Mars are produced by seasonal wind erosion. As first revealed during the *Viking* missions of the 1970s, violent "dust devils" commonly swirl across the surface, leaving in their wake various exposed types of rock minerals of differing colors, such as dark volcanic bedrock. The storms on Mars are always more frequent and intense when the planet's orbit brings it closer to the Sun, which would be Martian summer in the Southern Hemisphere.

Today, the camera aboard *Mars Global Surveyor*, the first spacecraft of NASA's Mars Exploration Program, launched on November 7, 1996, has captured numerous images of the Martian surface, including

ter life on Earth were not unique within the universe. To Sagan, this showed that the evolution of life on other worlds was possible, which led to the formulation of the new field of *exobiology*.

In 1954, due to the implications of the Miller-Urey experiment, Sagan wrote a thesis on the origins of life, and in 1955 he received his bachelor's degree in physics. The following year, he received his master's degree in the same discipline.

As a postgraduate, Sagan chose astronomy for his field of study. To get a better feel for what becoming an astronomer would

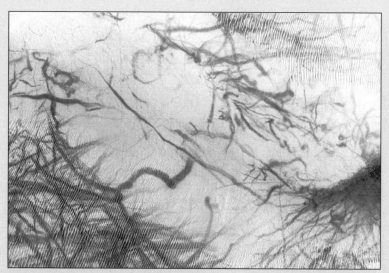

Martian Dust Devil Tracks. A view of the floor of Mars's Argyre Basin located around 48°S x 43°W showing numerous dark streaks thought to be created by the passage of dust devils *(Photo courtesy of NASA)*

ice-covered sands, blowing dunes, the changing shape of the southern ice cap, and huge, swirling dust devils towering as much as five miles (8 km) above the planet's surface. Further evidence suggests that at one time, liquid water coursed across the surface of Mars. This last evidence is an ongoing source of investigation and is the focus of current and future Mars missions.

involve, he set out in summer 1956 for McDonald Observatory in Fort Davis, Texas, and conducted his first true observation of Mars through the gigantic 82-inch (208 cm) telescope. To him, the sight of a tiny, washed-out tan dot was a disappointment. Especially since during that time in the late 1950s, there were still scientists tossing around the idea that the dark bands on Mars were green flora since they appeared to change their shape and size with the seasons, as plant life will do. In William M. Sinton's case, he called the features "Sinton bands," stating that when viewed through infrared, the dark bands on Mars were similar to those produced by organic compounds. Sagan clung to these familiar childhood theories until the final, disappointing proof came with the success of the *Mariner* missions that began in the 1960s.

The Unforgiving Search for Extraterrestrial Life

In 1956, Sagan met Lynn Alexander, a young biologist at the University of Chicago. The two married in 1957. In that same year, the couple moved to Madison, Wisconsin, where Sagan met American geneticist Joshua Lederberg, a scientist who in 1958 shared the Nobel Prize in physiology for his discoveries concerning genetic recombination and the organization of the genetic material of bacteria. (The other 1958 physiology winners were George Wells Beadle and Edward Lawrie Tatum.) Sagan and Lederberg agreed on many things concerning the future of science and the importance of exobiology, commonalities that formed the basis of a lasting relationship.

Meanwhile, the United States became suddenly more involved in rocketry and space exploration after the Russians put *Sputnik*, the first artificial Earth satellite, into orbit. This accomplishment by another nation intensified the ambition of U.S. space scientists to succeed in being the first to put a human into space. The Apollo program became the United States's political response to *Sputnik*, and the search for talent was on. In 1959, Sagan's first introduction to NASA arrived in the form of a letter from his friend Lederberg, who at the time was the newly appointed head of the National Academy of Sciences Space Science Board. Lederberg was seeking members to head the exobiology team for space probes. Carl Sagan was his first choice. Shortly before earning his doctorate, Sagan began work on this part-time NASA project to implement exobiology into the space program, backing Lederberg on his stand for the need to explore the Moon for evidence of past life. In June 1960, Sagan earned his doctorate in both astronomy and astrophysics.

In 1961, Sagan's first television appearance was on the news program *CBS Reports* among a panel of interviewees. The title of the

58-minute special was *Why Man in Space?* The documentary discussed topics regarding the U.S. space program and the problems it was facing putting a man in orbit. They talked about the concerns for astronaut health in space, the lack of adequate knowledge about the Moon and the rockets needed to get there, and about possible life on Mars. American astronaut John Glenn and Sagan's friend Lederberg were among the people interviewed.

In 1962, Sagan was offered an assistant professorship of astronomy at Harvard University and a position as astrophysicist at Smithsonian Astrophysical Observatory, both located in Cambridge, Massachusetts. He accepted both positions and began work as an astronomer, his boyhood dream. His love of exobiology, however, continued.

Then, in 1965, a year after its launch, the highly anticipated Mars mission probe *Mariner 4* sent back 21 photos that depicted a Martian landscape far removed from the one that exobiologists had hoped for. The planet appeared lifeless. Data also showed the atmospheric pressure of Mars, which was a startlingly low six millibars (Earth's is around 1,000 millibars). This pressure was not sufficient to support liquid water, which in that climate would either boil away or freeze, nor would it support life-forms of any kind. Mars was dry, desolate, and dead, with an atmosphere of mostly carbon dioxide. The planet was not pocked with swatches of green vegetation as Sagan had grown up believing. NASA cringed as the disappointing results were broadcast on network television to the American taxpayers, whose money largely funded NASA. The public was not happy at how its money was being spent. By the end of the year, the expectation of finding life on Mars was as dead as the planet itself.

Yet Sagan did not give up. For him, the search for extraterrestrial life had only just begun. Granted, there was apparently no life on Mars, but perhaps evidence of past life could be found. Then there was the vastness of space to consider. Sagan's interest in uncovering evidence of alien life did not focus purely on Mars. He argued that it was inconceivable that Earth could be the only planet capable of supporting life. Life was out there, perhaps even intelligent life, and it was simply a question of finding a means to contact them.

Contact beyond the Solar System

The following year, Sagan published his first science fiction book, *Planets* (1966), coauthored by Jonathan Norton Leonard, which fancifully described life on Jupiter. Sagan's invented, rather than factual, descriptions did little to impress his colleagues.

In 1971, Sagan left Harvard to accept a full professorship of astronomy at Cornell University in Ithaca, New York. In that same year, during a visit to NASA's Jet Propulsion Laboratory in Pasadena,

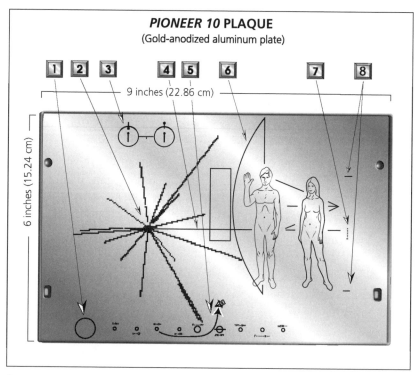

PIONEER 10 PLAQUE
(Gold-anodized aluminum plate)

1) Represents our solar system of the Sun and nine planets 2) Radial pattern indicating the position of our solar system and its distance away from certain pulsars in our galaxy 3) Illustrates a reverse of an electron's spin in a hydrogen atom, which emits a radio wave of 8.27 inches (21 cm) long, indicating that 8.27 inches is being used as our base length 4) Straight line indicating the distance from the Sun to the center of our galaxy 5) Trajectory of the *Pioneer* spacecraft as shown leaving from Earth, the third planet from the Sun 6) Silhouette of the *Pioneer* spacecraft 7) Vertical and horizontal ticks in binary code meaning the number eight 8) Bars showing the height of the woman compared to the spacecraft. By using the measurement formula of 8.27 inches multiplied by the binary number eight, the woman's height can be determined to be five feet, five inches (1.65 m).

California, concerning one of the Mars *Mariner* missions, freelance writers Eric Burgess and Richard Hoagland approached Sagan with the idea that a message should be placed aboard the *Pioneer 10* mission, which was slated for launch in March 1972. They reasoned that, once *Pioneer*'s job taking readings from Jupiter was completed, it would continue out of the solar system, becoming the first Earth probe to venture beyond the known planets into the unknowns of deep space without a set trajectory. *Pioneer 10* would continue to function for 20 or more years, since it was powered by radioisotope thermoelectric generators, or RTGs, which produce electricity from decaying plutonium. (RTGs are used when a spacecraft will be traveling too far from the Sun to warrant the use of solar power.) In other words, no one knew where it would end up; no one knew how many eons it would continue to "coast" in space; and no one knew what other beings it might meet out there—if any.

This seemed like the perfect opportunity to place upon the spacecraft a message for any encounters with unknown intelligent species that might answer questions as to where it came from and who sent it. Sagan agreed. He contacted NASA, and to his surprise, NASA agreed as well. The artistic designs for a plaque etched with a message were the responsibility of Sagan's new wife, Linda Salzman, whom he married in 1968 after having divorced Lynn Alexander in 1965.

Sagan also headed the projects of other interstellar messages sent out on the *Pioneer 11*, *Voyager I*, and *Voyager II* missions. When the *Voyager* missions launched in 1977, they each carried a gold-plated copper record containing much more information than the plaque fastened to the *Pioneer* probes. The two-hour-long record (played at 16 2/3 revolutions per minute) carried recorded pictures, convertible from audio to video; 87.5 minutes of music; sounds of nature, such as whale songs and erupting volcanoes; and greetings in 55 human languages, along with an excess of other data. A full account of the gold record, its contents and purposes, the people involved in its creation, and the missions of the *Voyager* spacecraft is in the 1978 book *Murmurs of the Earth: The Voyager Interstellar Record*, by Carl Sagan, F. D. Drake, Ann Druyan, Timothy Ferris, Jon Lomberg, and Linda Salzman Sagan.

The Champion of Space Science

Sagan's first appearance on the *Tonight Show with Johnny Carson* in 1973 was a five-minute slot at the end. He was a natural, very comfortable behind the camera, and had a way with words that caused the audience to watch, listen, and want to know more. He was so popular that Carson had him back three weeks later, which pleased the publishers of *The Cosmic Connection*, his 1973 book about the universe.

Cosmos

In the late 1970s, PBS devised a landmark science miniseries named *Cosmos*, hosted by celebrity scientist Carl Sagan. The series was created partly in answer to sophisticated BBC productions such as the award-winning *The Ascent of Man*. The goal of *Cosmos* was to introduce science to the mainstream community by explaining astrophysics, astronomy, cosmology, evolution, molecular biology, and the search for life beyond Earth in simplified terms via television. The $8 million in funding for the 13 one-hour episodes came from the Atlantic Richfield Company, the Corporation for Public Broadcasting, and the Arthur Vining Davis Foundations. Aside from Sagan's own production company called Carl Sagan Productions (formed after the disappointing coverage of the *Viking* missions to Mars) and KCET public television in California, coproducers were also the BBC and West Germany's Polytel International.

The original title considered for the show was *Man in the Cosmos;* however, Sagan's wife, Ann, regarded the title as sexist and suggested a change to simply *Cosmos*. The show's veteran producer was Adrian Malone, who produced *The Ascent of Man* and *The Age of Uncertainty*. He and Sagan hired special-effects artists who had worked

Following his experience on *The Tonight Show*, Sagan soon realized the potential of television as an educational tool. Many of his scientific peers scoffed at the concept of exobiology, but the public tended to be more open-minded. Realizing he would probably never find satisfactory support from within the science community, he decided to take his science and educate the populace. Television became a way for him to do that. Sagan approached exobiology with stubbornness and determination. He did not care about the more conservative views of other scientists or what they might be

on the movie *Star Wars* and computer graphics specialists from NASA's Jet Propulsion Laboratory. Shooting and production for *Cosmos* commenced in 1979, during which time the production staff consulted more than 100 different scientists concerning scientific accuracy and verification of facts. By September 1980, the show debuted on PBS, featuring the most extensive use of special effects ever in a documentary program. The theme music, composed by Vangelis and titled "Heaven and Hell—3rd Movement (Theme from the TV series 'Cosmos')" was as remarkable as the effects and later went on to become a popular soundtrack.

Throughout the show, Sagan used a stage designed to resemble the inside of a spaceship that he called "a ship of the imagination," and would feign using the ship's crystalline controls as he transported viewers on a cosmic voyage to explore pulsars, quasars, supernovas, the planets of our solar system, and to examine the potential of life beyond Earth.

As luck would have it, an actors' strike in 1980 forced networks into broadcasting reruns well into the fall season. Many viewers turned to PBS for fresh entertainment. *Cosmos* snared a great many viewers, received great ratings, and eventually won Emmy Awards (for excellence in the advancement of the arts and sciences of television) and Peabody Awards (recognizing outstanding achievement in electronic media, including radio, television, and cable). It was viewed by more than 500 million people in more than 60 countries. PBS still considers *Cosmos* its most popular broadcast.

saying about his work. Through the media, he sought to share his ideas with the public and lead them to explore the unexplored, ask the unasked, to prove that there are no embarrassing questions, and to show that there are no embarrassing subjects throughout the search for new knowledge.

By 1978, one year after he announced his divorce from Linda Salzman, Sagan had appeared frequently on television and was rapidly becoming a scientific celebrity. People loved him and he loved their attention. It was during this time that plans began for *Cosmos*, an ambitious 13-part PBS (Public Broadcasting Service) series on space hosted by Sagan. This was also when Sagan met Ann Druyan, a woman who later became his third wife and constant companion for the rest of his life. She was very involved with nearly everything Sagan did, from coauthoring *Comets* (1985) and *Shadows of Forgotten Ancestors* (1992), to giving valuable input regarding *Cosmos*, the television series.

Carl Sagan Is a Household Word

The success of *Cosmos* made Sagan a star. By the end of the 1970s, his name was synonymous with the now-popular subject of astronomy and the exciting potential for life beyond Earth. To accompany the television series, Sagan wrote a book, also titled Cosmos, which was published in 1980. The book was a huge success and stayed on the *New York Times* nonfiction bestseller list for more than a year. By the early 1980s, Carl Sagan was likely the most famous astronomer the world had ever known. He was on the October 20, 1980, cover of *Time* magazine in a feature article titled "Showman of Science." The month before, he was on the cover of *Sky and Telescope* magazine, photographed on the set of *Cosmos*, in a feature article titled "Carl Sagan's Voyage through the Cosmos." Some colleagues who had criticized him before now were humbled by his popularity and success, yet many were jealous and continued to scorn his work. Sagan ignored the backlash and forged ahead with his scientific goals.

After a brush with death in 1983, when he was hospitalized and nearly died from complications arising from an emergency appendectomy, Sagan became an integral part of a search program called SETI (Search for Extraterrestrial Intelligence). The SETI program

Deep Space Communication Antennae Array. The three Beam Waveguide antennas located at the Goldstone Deep Space Communications Complex in San Bernardino, California, are fine examples of a radio telescope array.

had been around since 1959, when the first search for sounds from space was conducted by Frank Drake, a friend and associate of Sagan, using a radio telescope. At that time, the SETI program was very small and funding was minimal. In 1984, SETI formed as a nonprofit society with the official purpose of conducting scientific research and educational projects in search of further life in the universe.

In 1985, NASA awarded SETI a research grant with plans to build a radio telescope of unparalleled proportions to be used exclusively in the search for extraterrestrial signals from space. Tragically for the program, funds were pulled, forcing NASA to scrap the project.

Fortunately for SETI, financial support came from the Planetary Society, which did not affiliate itself with the U.S. government or the taxpayers' money. The Planetary Society depends on contributions from memberships and other outside financial support. In 1980, Carl Sagan (the society's president), Louis Friedman, and Bruce Murray founded the Planetary Society with the purpose of encouraging the exploration of the solar system and the search for extraterrestrial life. The society received financial help from the noted Hollywood film director Steven Spielberg, who remains on the Planetary Society's board of directors to this day.

Another highlight in Sagan's life was the 1985 release of his book *Contact*, a fictional adventure story about a team of research scientists who, after years of scanning space, began to receive messages from another world. The team attempts to contact the source of the message through the use of an innovative spacecraft and is rewarded with a surprising result. The book was not as successful as *Cosmos*, but it was made into a Hollywood movie directed by Robert Zemeckis and starring Jodie Foster. The movie debuted in 1997 but, tragically, Carl Sagan did not live long enough to see the final cut.

One day in 1994, Sagan's wife noticed a bruise on his arm that was not healing. He underwent a routine blood test and discovered he had myelodysplasia, a bone marrow disease. He was informed that he would need a bone marrow transplant. In March 1995, he was admitted to Seattle's Fred Hutchison Cancer Research Center for treatment. His sister Carol was called upon to donate matching bone marrow. At age 60, Sagan became the eldest recipient thus far to undergo this type of transplant. By August 1995, Sagan was on his feet again, doing speeches and attending symposiums, but by December, as production for the film *Contact* progressed, the doctors found evidence that the disease was resurfacing. Sagan began a series of chemotherapy treatments and received another transplant from Carol.

Sagan bounced back from the second surgery, and his last book, *The Demon-Haunted World: Science as a Candle in the Dark* (1996), which focused on the differences between "true science" and "artificial science," was published and drew favorable reviews. He was also working on a novel titled *Billions and Billions: Thoughts on Life and Death at the Brink of the Millennium*, putting together a collection of essays covering a wide variety of topics, including life on Mars, global warming, the invention of chess, and his fight with bone marrow disease. It was not long, however, before his disease recurred. Carl Sagan died of pneumonia in Seattle on December 20, 1996.

Sagan's Legacy

Throughout his career, there was very little that concerned space and astronomy in which Carl Sagan was not involved. He delved into areas of planetary exploration, life in the cosmos, science education, and public policy and government regulation of science and the environment. Sagan won the Pulitzer Prize for literature in 1978 for *The Dragons of Eden: Speculations on the Evolution of Human Intelligence* (1977). He published more than 600 scientific papers and articles and authored, coauthored, and edited more than 20 books.

Aside from being a prolific writer, he was involved in the NASA space program from the very beginning, including the *Mariner*, *Pioneer*, *Viking*, *Voyager*, and *Galileo* expeditions to other planets between the 1960s and the 1990s. He received a medal for exceptional scientific achievement, two for distinguished public service, and also the NASA Apollo Achievement Award, among many others. Colleges and universities across the United States also bestowed more than 20 medals and awards on Sagan for his contributions to science, literature, and education, but he may be remembered best for his public image.

Carl Sagan's success can be attributed to many things, including his ambition, intelligence, and good timing as far as the blossoming U.S. space program was concerned, but it was his uncommon gift for communication that gained him the public role he played within his chosen profession. There is no doubt that Carl Sagan's lifework will influence the world community in the generations to come. It would be very appropriate to think of Carl Sagan as the people's astronomer.

CHRONOLOGY

1934	Born on November 9 in Brooklyn, New York
1939	Visits the New York World's Fair, which makes a lasting impression on his thoughts toward science
1951	Enters the University of Chicago on scholarship
1952–53	Meets Nobel Prize–winning American geneticists Herrmann Muller and Harold Urey, and learns of Stuart Miller and the Miller-Urey experiment. The new field of exobiology is born.
1955	Receives a bachelor's degree in physics from the University of Chicago

1956	Receives a master's degree in physics from the University of Chicago and a National Science Foundation predoctoral fellowship
1959	Asked to be a leading member of a special NASA committee to implement exobiology into the space program
1960	earns a doctorate in astrophysics and astronomy from the University of Chicago
1962	Begins teaching as an assistant professor of astronomy at Harvard University and starts work as an astrophysicist at the Smithsonian Observatory
1965	*Mariner 4* sends back the first good photos of Mars, showing a planet devoid of vegetation of any kind
1966	Publishes *Planets,* his first nontechnical book
1971	Becomes professor of astronomy at Cornell University
1972	*Pioneer 10* launches for Jupiter, carrying within it Sagan's gold plaque engraved with greetings from Earth
1973	Makes his first appearance on *The Tonight Show,* promoting his upcoming book, *The Cosmic Connection*
1977	The *Voyager* missions launch in summer, each carrying a gold-plated record with messages from Earth
1979	Shooting and production begins on television series *Cosmos*
1980	*Cosmos* airs on September 28. Sagan cofounds the Planetary Society with Louis Friedman and Bruce Murray, and becomes its first president
1984	Helps found the SETI Institute (Search for Extraterrestrial Intelligence)
1994	Is diagnosed with bone marrow disease
1996	Dies on December 20 in Seattle, Washington
1997	His book *Billions and Billions* is published posthumously

FURTHER READING

Books

Cohen, Daniel. *Carl Sagan: Superstar Scientist.* New York: Dodd, Mead, 1987. A biography of Carl Sagan's career written for younger readers.

Davidson, Keay. *Carl Sagan: A Life.* Hoboken, N.J.: John Wiley & Sons, 2000. A finely researched biography on the successes and controversies surrounding Carl Sagan and his illustrious public career.

Poundstone, William. *Carl Sagan: A Life in the Cosmos.* New York: Henry Holt, 1999. A comprehensive biography of Carl Sagan, ranging from his childhood to events after his death.

Sagan, Carl. *Cosmos.* New York: Random House, 1980. A companion book based on the award-winning 1970s TV series of the same name, covering 15 billion years of cosmic evolution. It spent 72 weeks on the *New York Times* best-seller list.

———. *The Dragons of Eden: Speculations on the Evolution of Human Intelligence.* New York: Ballantine Books, 1986. Sagan's Pulitzer Prize–winning book that takes the reader through a history of the origins of human intelligence.

———, and I. S. Shklovskii. *Intelligent Life in the Universe.* New York: Random House, 1966. At nearly 40 years old, this volume stills holds a surprising amount of useful information discussing the scientific possibilities of life in the cosmos. It is a fine example of Carl Sagan's compelling writing style.

Web Sites

SETI (Search for Extraterrestrial Intelligence.) Available online. URL: http://www.seti-inst.edu. Accessed November 29, 2004. The mission of the SETI Institute is to explore, understand, and explain the origin, nature, and prevalence of life in the universe. Web site offers membership, media information, SETI news, events calendar, featured topics, and announcements.

10

Stephen Hawking

(1942–)

Stephen Hawking has been compared to Albert Einstein. *(Photo courtesy of AIP Emilio Segrè Visual Archives, Physics Today Collection)*

The Modern Einstein

The British theoretical physicist Stephen Hawking is one of the world's top modern scientists. Many believe him to be the most brilliant scientist since American physicist Albert Einstein (1879–1955). Undeterred by a crippling motor neuron disease, Hawking conducts pioneering research into the origin of the universe and has worked toward combining quantum mechanics and gravity into a unified theory, which would incorporate all basic interactions between matter and energy. This combined theory is particularly crucial to the formation of cosmological models of the early universe, Hawking's specialty. He has made groundbreaking discoveries toward proving the existence of *black holes* and describing their characteristics, which includes radiation emission. He is perhaps most famous for working to make complex cosmological theories comprehensible to the public through books, films, and lectures.

An Unusual Birthday

Stephen William Hawking was born on January 8, 1942, in Oxford, England, exactly 300 years to the day after the death of famous Italian astronomer Galileo Galilei (1564–1642). Stephen's father, Frank Hawking, was a doctor specializing in tropical diseases. His mother, Isobel, worked as a medical secretary before she was married. Stephen was the eldest child in the Hawking family. He had two biological sisters, Mary and Philippa, and an adopted brother, Edward.

In 1950, the family moved to St. Albans, a city in Hertfordshire, a county in southeastern England. In 1952, Stephen enrolled at St. Albans private school for boys, where his teachers came to know him as a very bright if rather clumsy boy. He was thin, poor at ball games, had atrocious handwriting, and excelled in academia, especially mathematics. Stephen's social peers were the brightest boys at the school. Together they liked to experiment with electronics and model aviation and held deep intellectual discussions on everything from religion to politics. Through these discussions, Stephen came to realize he had a penchant for rational logic, which helped to mold him into the brilliant theorist he would someday become.

Talent and Scholarship

By the time he was 14, Stephen realized he wanted to pursue a career in mathematics. He discovered he was able to quickly formulate an answer to a mathematical problem while others were still trying to begin. Solving equations was intuitive to him. Stephen was one of those rare students who appeared to never have to study and still received the highest marks.

In 1959, he took the entrance exams for University College, Oxford, with the intent of studying physics, known during that time as the natural sciences. University College did not offer courses in mathematics. Stephen's father preferred that he take up studies in chemistry and medicine, but Stephen convincingly argued that mathematics was what he was best at; it was what he loved. Within a few days after the completion of his exams and interviews, Hawking was accepted and awarded a scholarship at University College.

By 1962, he received a bachelor's degree in physics. Hawking then transferred to Cambridge University to pursue a doctorate. He began his studies in cosmology and general relativity, a field that was lacking in development and therefore the most attractive to Hawking. His hope was to study under Fred Hoyle, Britain's most distinguished astronomer of the time. Instead, Hawking studied under Dennis Sciama, who turned out to be a superb scientist and associate. Sciama's job as supervisor was to help Hawking find a research niche; however, it did not take long for Sciama to notice that Hawking was struggling with something other than finding a suitable study assignment.

Tragedy, Heartbreak, and Depression

In December 1962, Hawking traveled home to St. Albans for Christmas. While he was still in Oxford, Hawking had begun to experience increasing episodes of physical awkwardness. He kept bumping into things and had trouble with simple motor skills, such as tying his shoes. Occasionally, he would experience slurred speech, and on two or three rare occasions, he fell to the ground without any apparent cause. To Hawking, these symptoms came on gradually and were easy to dismiss, yet when he visited his family, whom he had not seen for months, they instantly noticed the change.

Appointments were made with a doctor, then a specialist. After all the tests came back, it was learned that Hawking had an incurable motor neuron disease known as amyotrophic lateral sclerosis (ALS). In the United States, it is known as Lou Gehrig's disease, after a famous New York Yankees baseball player from the 1920s–30s who contracted the disease and quit baseball in 1939. The specialists gave Hawking two years to live.

Hawking fell into a state of depression. How could he finish his doctorate now? His studies suffered, and he wondered why he had been dealt such a devastating blow. For a while, he shut himself away and drowned his troubles listening to the music of Wagner.

Turning Point

Once the disease took hold, Hawking's condition quickly deteriorated. He soon began to rely on a walking stick to help him move about. He acted confused and behaved as if there were no point in living.

His salvation came, not only from the strong will lying dormant within him, but also in the form of Jane Wilde, a girl he met and became acquainted with during the 1962 holiday festivities at his parents' home. He and Jane announced their engagement, and Hawking returned to his routine with more pleasure and a better work ethic than ever before.

With a Ph.D. as his goal, Hawking moved forward under Sciama, attending lectures and seminars that would conclude in open discussion. Soon he became involved in the first publicly important project of his undergraduate years. At Cambridge, students' work was never secretive. After examining the work being done by one of Fred Hoyle's students, Jayant Narlikar, on Hoyle's steady-state theory of the origins of the universe, Hawking began, out of sheer fascination, to formulate a theory of his own. According to Hawking in a January 2002 article in *Plus Magazine* titled "Sixty Years in a Nutshell," the steady-state theory is:

> . . . one in which as the universe expanded, new matter was continually created to keep the density constant on average. The steady state theory was never on a very strong theoretical basis, because it required a negative energy field to create the matter. This would have made it unstable to runaway production of matter and negative energy. But it had the great merit as a scientific theory, of making definite predictions that could be tested by observations.

On one memorable occasion, Hawking attended a lecture given by Hoyle on his steady-state theory, during which Hoyle provided a premature mathematical model consistent with the general theory of relativity. As usual, attendees joined in discussion after the lecture. In a room full of scientists, Hawking stood and challenged Hoyle, claiming that he was announcing results not yet verified. Hawking insisted that Hoyle's quantity diverged; that the influence of all the matter in a steady-state universe would make his masses infinite. Hawking later proved himself right by showing his mathematical findings in writing, which he had calculated before Hoyle's lecture. His findings were highly received and, at the very least, they characterized Hawking as Hoyle's intellectual equal.

Singularity Theory and the Universe

An important question in the minds of 20th-century scientists was: did the universe have a beginning? The general theory of relativity predicted that it should, but provided no real proof. Hawking regularly attended lectures at London's Kings College. After one lecture given by British mathematician Roger Penrose, who discussed the possibility of a space-time *singularity* at the center of a black hole, Hawking began to consider the idea of applying the same *space-time* singularity theory to the universe. This would not be easy, yet Hawking did it since he was desperately looking for something on which to complete his thesis. The last part of his doctoral thesis described the application of the singularity theory on the universe, a breakdown in space and time where the common laws of physics would no longer apply. In 1965, he received a doctorate in theoretical physics. Shortly thereafter, he and Jane married. They would eventually have three children, Robert, Lucy, and Timothy.

That same year, Gonville and Caius College, Cambridge, awarded Hawking a research fellowship. By this time, he had outlived his predicted life expectancy, yet his health was growing worse. He no longer had the ability to write by hand, and his speech became increasingly slurred. Hawking made light of his condition and never failed to find ways to overcome the aspects of his disability. In December 1965, he attended a relativity meeting in Miami, where he was to deliver a public lecture about his singularity theory. Through the aid of George Ellis, an old friend who agreed to do the speaking for Hawking, the lecture was highly received by the prominent scientists attending. His reputation as a renowned physicist was mounting.

General Theory of Relativity

In 1915, the American physicist Albert Einstein first proposed the general theory of relativity as an extension from his earlier special theory of relativity. Though mathematically complex, the general theory of relativity is based on a single principle called equivalence. Simply stated, equivalence makes gravitational acceleration and mechanical acceleration indistinguishable when described mathematically. For an example, if an astronaut in space accelerates in a rocket ship, the astronaut would be able to feel his or her body "weight." The perceived weight depends on the rate of acceleration, meaning if the rocket accelerates at the same rate as the Earth's natural acceleration due to gravity, the astronaut will "weigh" the same as on Earth. The theory also proposes that light will "bend" around a massive object, such as a star. In 1919, scientists conducted the first test of the general theory of relativity when they correctly predicted the timing of Mercury's transit across the Sun, proving that the light path had been "bent" by the Sun's gravitational field.

As research fellow, Hawking continued his work on his singularity theory. In 1966, he wrote an essay called "Singularities and the Geometry of Spacetime," which earned him the Adams Prize, Cambridge University's most prestigious mathematical award. By this time, Hawking was in collaboration with Roger Penrose, now a mathematics professor at Birkbeck College, London. Together they worked on devising new mathematical techniques in order to carry out the necessary calculations that would aid in verifying their theory that the universe began as a singularity. The combined talents of the two scientists made it possible for them to produce reliable data concerning what is known as the big bang theory. In 1970, Hawking and

The Big Bang Theory

In 1927, the Belgian astronomer Georges Lemaître (1894–1966) first introduced the theory of an expanding universe. In a paper entitled "Primitive Atom," Lemaître explained that as one travels further back in time, the closer the galaxies become until the universe is eventually compressed into a single atom. The explosion of this atom caused the universe to expand and grow. Years later, the American astronomer Edwin Hubble (1889–1953) provided evidence in support of Lemaître by showing that distant galaxies in every direction are traveling away from us with speeds proportional to their distance. This expansion of the majority of observed galaxies implies that at some time in the distant past, the galaxies were indeed very close together.

Professor Fred Hoyle from the University of Cambridge first coined the term *big bang* during a 1950 BBC radio program called *The Nature of the Universe*, intending it as a joke to ridicule the idea of an expanding universe and make his steady-state theory seem more attractive. To his dismay, the term stuck.

The big bang theory proposes that roughly 15 billion years ago the universe did not exist, nor did space and time. Then an infinitely dense explosion of immeasurable temperature burst from the confines of a single point (a singularity), bringing about the birth of matter, energy, and space and time. Universal particles began a great rate of expansion, and in a fraction of a second, the universe grew hundreds of times in size. Within three minutes, temperatures began to cool and protons and neutrons slowed down enough to allow the assembly of elements. Much later, galaxies formed as the universe continued to expand to its present size and state. The universe could continue its expansion forever or contract again into another big bang.

Penrose published a paper in support of the big bang theory entitled "The Singularities of Gravitational Collapse and Cosmology," which proved that if general relativity is true and the universe is expanding, a singularity must have occurred at the birth of the universe.

Theory on Black Holes

In 1973, Hawking left Gonville and Caius College and joined the department of applied mathematics and theoretical physics, known as DAMPT, at Cambridge University. In this same year, Hawking published *The Large Scale Structure of Spacetime*, which was a complex collaboration between him and associate George Ellis dealing with classical cosmology. By now, Hawking relied upon a wheelchair, though this did not hinder his career. His mind was the most important tool he needed. For everything else there was help, be it in the form of a wheelchair or, as the future would hold, a computerized speech device.

Another major contribution made by Hawking was his work on black holes. (In 1969, American theoretical physicist John Wheeler had first coined the term *black hole*.) The knowledge of the existence

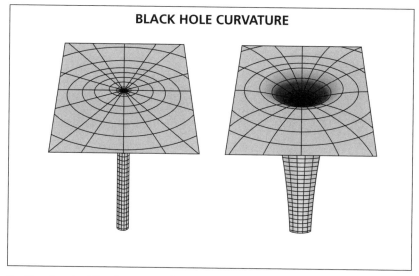

BLACK HOLE CURVATURE

Hawking theorized that in an expanding universe, black holes could occur in different sizes. The drawing on the left is of a small black hole with a sudden curvature. The drawing on the right is of a large black hole with a gradual curvature.

of a "dark star"—a region of space thought to be so grossly warped by gravitational forces that nothing could escape from it, not even light—had been around for about two centuries. In 1796, the French scientist Pierre-Simon Laplace (1749–1827), working from Newton's theory of gravitation, theorized that since light consisted of particles it must therefore be affected by gravity. Laplace put forward that some stars may be too massive to radiate and that the largest bodies in the universe may be invisible.

The boundary of a black hole from which nothing can escape is known as the event horizon. For years, the conjecture has been that all light and matter that falls past the event horizon and into the black hole is lost forever. During the early 1970s, in a wave of revolutionary research, Hawking showed that that was not the case and that black holes in fact emit radiation. He also theorized that since they were emitting particles, they were also losing mass and would therefore eventually cease to exist. He came to this theory by combining three very different areas of physics: that of general relativity—which describes gravity and the very large—that of quan-

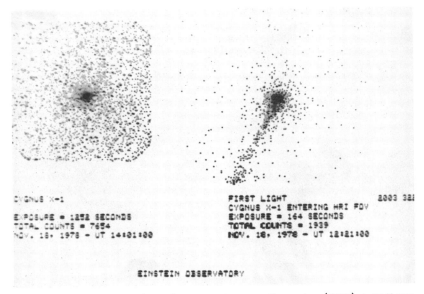

In 1978, the first object seen by High Energy Astronomy Observatory (HEAO)—2, an X-ray space telescope also known as the Einstein Observatory, was of a possible black hole in the constellation Cygnus. Named Cygnus X-1, this is the first black hole ever discovered. The color in this image is reversed for clarity. (Photo courtesy of NASA-MSFC)

tum mechanics—which describes particles and the very small—and that of thermodynamics—heat theory—to form a single theory. Hawking's findings provided the first positive steps toward suggesting a unity in the separate branches of physics, something scientists had been trying to do for the past 50 years. Hawking also put forth that because of the big bang theory, black holes could have an alternative beginning (other than stellar collapse) and that they could be of varying sizes. Before Hawking, the common thinking was that the creation of a huge black hole occurred when a dead star too heavy to be a neutron star collapsed under the force of its own gravity. Hawking suggested that the big bang expansion of the universe could squeeze pockets of matter into "primordial black holes" that could have a mass as little as roughly 10^{-5} gram.

At first, as with many scientific breakthroughs, Hawking's discovery concerning the properties of black holes was not broadly accepted, and it caused widespread controversy throughout the scientific community. Eventually, the controversy grew into acceptance. The radiation emitted by black holes is now known as Hawking radiation. Originally identified in 1965 as an X-ray source, Cygnus X-1 was identified in 1978 by the Einstein Observatory as the first possible candidate for being a black hole.

Cosmology Stardom

Within the rapidly advancing world of modern technology, the name Stephen Hawking was becoming synonymous with innovative cosmology and the mysterious and intriguing issue of black holes. Recognition for his talent was coming fast upon him. In March 1974, Hawking became one of the youngest scientists elected to the Royal Society of London. Between 1975 and 1976, he won six awards for his advances in science, including the Eddington Medal from the Royal Astronomical Society, the Pius XI Medal from the Vatican Pontifical Academy of Science, the William Hopkins Prize from the Cambridge Philosophical Society, the Hughes Medal from the Royal Society of London, the Dannie Heinemann Prize, and the Maxwell Prize.

In 1977, Cambridge created a special chair of gravitational physics exclusively for Hawking, to hold for as long as he remains at the university. In 1978, he received the prestigious Albert Einstein World Award of Science given by the Lewis and Rose Strauss Memorial Fund in recognition of his work toward unifying physics. Then, in 1979, one of the highlights in Hawking's life occurred when he became Lucasian professor of mathematics at Cambridge University, a position of high honor first held in 1663 by English mathemetician Isaac Barrow (1630–77) and then by English physicist Isaac Newton (1642–1727) in 1669.

Though burdened with the duties of professorship and travel associated with his growing celebrity, Hawking was able to carry on with his theoretical work. By 1981, he had published a book on cosmology with Martin Rocek called *Superspace and Supergravity.* In December 1981, Queen Elizabeth II honored Hawking by naming him a Commander of the British Empire.

In 1983, Hawking, Gary W. Gibbons, and T. C. Silkos published a book called *The Very Early Universe*, describing the big bang theory in complex terms. In the meantime, New York University, the University of Notre Dame, Princeton University, and Britain's University of Leicester each made him an honorary doctor of science. Also in 1983, the BBC (British Broadcasting Corporation) profiled Hawking in a program called *Horizon*, where he was shown going about his business at the DAMPT at Cambridge. Hawking welcomed the publicity.

A Brief History of Time

Not long after the publication of *The Very Early Universe*, Hawking decided to write a book on cosmology that would appeal to the general public. The title of the book was *A Brief History of Time: From the Big Bang to Black Holes.* An unfortunate delay of the book's final draft occurred in 1985, when Hawking contracted pneumonia while visiting CERN (Centre Européen pour la Recherche Nucléaire/European Organization for Nuclear Research) a particle physics laboratory in Geneva, Switzerland. Extremely ill, Hawking was flown to Addenbrooke's Hospital at Cambridge University, where surgeons performed a tracheotomy. The operation saved his life but denied him any further use of his voice. Hawking adopted a small computer device linked to his wheelchair that synthesized speech through commands he made with his hand. This was far less convenient for Hawking; however, it turned out to be a better situation for the people who previously had a hard time comprehending him. Before the speech synthesizer, only those closest to him could understand his speech.

Hawking's *A Brief History of Time* was finally published in 1988 and remained on *The New York Times* best-seller list for a record-breaking 234 weeks. Within its pages, Hawking delved into the known theories of the cosmos with all its unresolved conflicts and addressed the problem of unifying quantum mechanics, thermodynamics, and general relativity; however, the defining characteristic of this book was that it made possible for the average reader with an interest in cosmology to understand the theories and mathematics involved. Even today, *A Brief History of Time* remains one of the best-selling books of all time.

Scientific Icon

Hawking has been the subject of numerous documentaries about his life. For example, he was the focus of a BBC program called *Master of the Universe*, which in 1990 won Britain's Royal Television Society award. Hawking also appeared in the United States on ABC's *20/20*. During this time, Hawking continued to be the recipient of awards. In 1988, he and Roger Penrose accepted the Israeli Wolf Foundation Prize for their work on black holes. Then, in 1989, Queen Elizabeth II made him a Companion of Honor. In this same year, he received an honorary doctor of science award from Cambridge University. This is considered a very high honor, and it is a rare event for a professor to receive this award from his or her own university.

In 1990, noted American filmmaker Errol Morris became interested in doing a high-budget television special about Hawking's life called *A Brief History of Time*. It debuted in 1991. The 80-minute film included interviews with Hawking as well as many of his immediate family members, neighbors, classmates, professors, and scientific colleagues. Although the documentary had the same name as Hawking's book, the film included more commentary about Hawking than it did about the physics of his work. In summer 1991, Hawking and his wife, Jane separated. Two years later, he published a collection of essays entitled *Black Holes and Baby Universes*, a work that embraced aspects of astrophysics as well as his own personal life. Hawking married again in 1995, to Elaine Mason, his longtime nurse.

Calling for the Death of Physics

Throughout the mid-1990s, some of Hawking's focus shifted to the investigation of the Einstein-Rosen bridge, also known as *wormholes* or tunnels through space-time, and the question of whether time travel is possible. The prospect of time travel intrigued Kip Thorn, a theorist at Caltech (California Institute of Technology), as well as other eminent scientists. Thorn and his colleagues showed that general relativity allows for the possibility of a particular type of wormhole to exist as a cosmic connection between two black holes. Thus, it appears to be mathematically feasible for matter to travel through a wormhole (when the tunnel is momentarily open) and potentially arrive at the other end in another part of the universe. In other words, Thorne put forth that no evidence exists that specifically forbids the possibility of time travel. Hawking used an obvious question to argue against the reality of time travel by asking that, if it were indeed possible, why were future time travelers not here today educating us about it?

In 1996, Hawking published *The Illustrated Brief History of Time*, a very different book compared to his 1988 work of similar title, with the addition of more than 240 color illustrations and images. One completely new chapter discusses wormholes and possible resolutions to the classic paradoxes surrounding time travel.

His latest book, called *The Universe in a Nutshell*, was published in 2001. Hawking designed this cosmology book so that readers could go to any chapter of their choice, after fully reading chapters one and two, and comprehend a chosen topic without having to wade through successive chapters that might not be of immediate interest.

Although he is a devoted family man, research continues to dominate Hawking's life, and he enjoys placing wagers on the outcome of current cosmological research. For example, in 1997 Hawking and Thorne joined forces and wagered against Caltech theorist John Preskill that black holes cannot emit data, only thermal radiation, which contains no data. Preskill argued that black holes could indeed emit data, and the race for an answer was on. Upon the resolution to the problem, the winner was to provide the loser with an encyclopedia of their choice. In 2004, during the International Conference on General Relativity in Dublin, Ireland, Hawking conceded defeat by stating he found that black holes do indeed emit data, not just heat. He explained that when performing a path integral on a black hole of a particular shape, data is not lost but is instead allowed to escape through an "apparent" horizon, which is present due to the improper formation of a true event horizon. Though Hawking lost the bet, his work was another step toward a unified theory.

A life dedicated to science is not an easy one, especially when faced with above-average challenges such as those faced by Stephen Hawking. Ironically, Hawking claims that because of his disability he has perhaps been allowed far greater time to think than other scientists. The quest for answers about the creation of the universe has been the motivation in Hawking's career and is perhaps responsible for his surviving decades beyond the life expectancy given him by his doctors. He has dedicated his talents toward uncovering a scientific theory that can explain everything about the cosmos, and he continues to be a part of new theories and discoveries. By merging quantum mechanics and general relativity, Hawking is calling for the death of classical physics in favor of a unified quantum theory of gravity with the goal of producing solid evidence on how the universe began. Few people fully understand the complexities of Hawking's work, yet he has succeeded in describing the otherwise indescribable to millions, in itself a major accomplishment. Due to his scientific achievements and literary contributions, a diverse numbers of people now hope that someday, whether through Hawking or other future pioneers in science, the secrets of the universe can be unmistakably clear.

CHRONOLOGY

1942	Stephen William Hawking is born on January 8 in Oxford, England
1952	Begins private school at St. Albans and realizes his talent for logic and mathematics

1959	Receives a scholarship to University College, Oxford
1962	Earns a bachelor's degree in physics from Oxford; enters Cambridge University to study cosmology
1963	Diagnosed with ALS (amyotrophic lateral sclerosis), a motor neuron disease
1965	Earns a doctorate in theoretical physics; awarded a research fellowship from Gonville and Caius College, Cambridge; marries Jane Wilde
1966	Writes an essay called "Singularities and the Geometry of Spacetime," which earns him the Adams Prize in mathematics
1970	Publishes "The Singularities of Gravitational Collapse and Cosmology" with Roger Penrose, proving that the big bang contained a singularity
1973	Joins the mathematics and theoretical physics department at Cambridge University; applies theories from general relativity, quantum physics, and thermodynamics to prove for the first time that black holes emit radiation
1974	Becomes a fellow of th Royal Society of London
1975–76	Earns six awards: the Eddington Medal, the Pius XI Medal, the William Hopkins Prize, the Dannie Heinemann Prize, the Maxwell Prize, and the Hughes Medal
1977	Cambridge University creates a special chair of gravitational physics exclusively for Hawking
1978	The first image of a possible black hole, called Cygnus X-1, is taken by HEAO-2 (High Energy Astronomy Observatory), the world's first X-ray space telescope. Hawking receives the Albert Einstein Award for his work toward unifying physics.
1979	Appointed Lucasian professor of mathematics at Cambridge University
1981	Publishes, with Martin Rocek, *Superspace and Supergravity,* a book that deals with cosmology; receives the royal CBE (Commander of the British Empire) award

1983	Publishes, with Gary W. Gibbons and T.C. Silkos, *The Very Early Universe,* describing the big bang theory in complex terms
1985	Contracts pneumonia while visiting CERN (Centre Européen pour la Recherche Nucléaire/European Organization for Nuclear Research), a particle physics laboratory in Geneva, Switzerland, resulting in the permanent loss of his voice
1988	Publishes the book for which he is most famous, *A Brief History of Time: From the Big Bang to Black Holes,* intended for the average reader interested in cosmology
1989	Made a Companion of Honor by Britain's Queen Elizabeth II
1991	Hollywood releases a documentary about Hawking's life, *A Brief History of Time.* He separates from his wife, Jane.
1992	Elected to the National Academy of Sciences
1993	Publishes a collection of essays entitled *Black Holes and Baby Universes,* containing astrophysical and autobiographical material
1995	Marries Elaine Mason
1996	Publishes *The Illustrated Brief History of Time,* in which he discusses time travel
2001	Publishes *The Universe in a Nutshell,* describing the concepts behind the theories of the birth and life of the universe
2004	Admits defeat over a bet made with Kip Thorne against John Preskill by showing that black holes do in fact emit data

FURTHER READING

Books

Boslough, John. *Stephen Hawking's Universe.* New York: Avon Books, 1989. A good book for the scientific layperson that discusses the big bang theory, pulsars, quasars, and black holes.

Hawking, Stephen. *A Brief History of Time: The Updated and Expanded Tenth Anniversary Edition.* New York: Bantam, 1998. Explores theories of the cosmos; updated and illustrated to embrace advances in research, including a new introduction and new chapters on wormholes and time travel.

————. *Black Holes and Baby Universes.* New York: Bantam, 1993. A collection of essays with topics ranging from autobiographical information to the concept of imaginary time. A good companion to Hawking's *A Brief History of Time.*

————. *The Universe in a Nutshell.* New York: Bantam, 2001. Written as a companion to *A Brief History of Time*, this book guides the reader on a space-time journey when the universe begins as a cosmic seed.

Wald, Robert M. *Space, Time, and Gravity: The Theory of the Big Bang and Black Holes.* 2d ed. Chicago: University of Chicago Press, 1992. Written for the layperson, this work addresses the physics of cosmology and black holes.

Weinberg, Steven. *The First Three Minutes: A Modern View of the Origins of the Universe.* New York: Bantam, 1979. Classic description of the early stages of the big bang theory and the highly dense state in which the universe began.

White, Michael, and John Gribbin. *Stephen Hawking: A Life in Science.* 3d ed. Washington, D.C.: Joseph Henry Press, 2002. An excellent look at Stephen Hawking's personal and professional life written in compelling style.

Web Sites

Plus Magazine. "Stephen Hawking's 60 Years in a Nutshell." Hawking, Stephen. Available online. URL: http://plus.maths.org/issue18/features/hawking. Accessed November 29, 2004. An article originally presented as a lecture by Hawking at the Center for Mathematical Sciences, Cambridge, England.

Stephen Hawking Official Web Site. Available online. URL: http://www.hawking.org.uk. Accessed November 29, 2004. The World Wide Web home page of Professor Stephen Hawking with information on his life, disability and current health, lectures, news, a glossary of terms, and how to contact him.

GLOSSARY

ablation   dispersion of heat using a consumptive process

abort   in aeronautics, to cut short or cancel a flight after it has been launched

aerodynamic heating   surface heating of a body caused by air friction and compression processes on passage of air or other gases over the body, significant largely at high speeds

aerodynamics   the science of motion through air and other gaseous media and the forces acting on bodies moving through such media

aerospace   Earth's atmospheric envelope and the space beyond, domain of operations for airborne vehicles, rockets, and spacecraft

albedo   a ratio of an object's reflected energy versus the total incident energy

apapsis   an object's farthest point from whatever object it is orbiting

aphelion   specific to an object's farthest point from the Sun in its orbit

apogee   specific to an object's farthest point from the Earth in its orbit

arc minute   an angular unit of measurement equal to one-sixtieth of a degree, of which there are 360 degrees in a circle

arc second   equal to one-sixtieth of an arc minute

astrology   a pseudo (artificial) science based on the belief that the locations of the Sun and planets will affect the outcome of human affairs

astronaut   a person who occupies a space vehicle

astronautics   the science of space flight, including the art, skill, or activity of operating space vehicles

astronomical unit (AU)   the average distance between the Earth and the Sun equal to 93,000,000 miles (150 million km), typically used as a unit of measurement within our solar system. Light travels one AU in 8.3 minutes.

astronomy   the science of studying celestial objects and the universe in which they exist

atmosphere   the envelope of air, or body of gases, surrounding the Earth or any other planetary or celestial body

attitude   in space science, this refers to the particular alignment of a spacecraft to its direction of motion

ballistic trajectory   the path followed by a body under the action of gravitational forces and the resistance of the medium through which it passes

binary star   two stars that rotate around a common center of mass, as opposed to double stars, which appear close in the sky but have no physical connection

blackbody   in physics, a theoretical object that absorbs all the electromagnetic radiation that it encounters

black hole   a region of space-time from which nothing, including light, can escape because of a strong gravitational field

capsule   a small, sealed, pressurized cabin with an internal environment capable of supporting human or animal life during extremely high altitude flight or space flight

celestial equator   the projection of the Earth's equator onto the celestial sphere

celestial poles   the projection of the Earth's poles onto the celestial sphere

celestial sphere   an infinite imaginary sphere within which all celestial objects appear to reside with the Earth at its center

collimate   in optics, the process of aligning the components (mirrors or lenses) of a telescope

command module   the section of a spacecraft where the astronauts live and operate the flight controls

cryogenics   pertaining to the storage of liquid fuels and oxidizers, cryogenics is the science of producing and maintaining very low temperatures

declination   the angular distance of a celestial object north or south of the celestial equator

eccentricity   refers to the measurement of an orbiting object's deviation from a circular orbit

eclipse   from the observer's perspective, this occurs when one celestial object passes in front of another, resulting in a shadow on the object's surface

ecliptic   the imaginary line that travels out from a circle in the celestial sphere where the Sun and planets are found in the sky

ephemeris   a table published usually for one calendar year that contains celestial information, such as daily predictions and locations for the phases of the Moon, bright stars, and planets for various locations on Earth

escape velocity   the particular velocity needed for a spacecraft or object to completely escape the gravitational pull of the Earth, Moon, or other massive body

exobiology   a branch of science that deals with the search for life outside of the Earth

finder   a much smaller telescope mounted on the body of a larger telescope to help an observer locate objects in the sky

focal length   the distance from the lens or mirror of a telescope to the location at which it focuses incident light

geocentric   another word for "Earth-centered." The prefix *geo-* is Greek for "Earth."

geosynchronous orbit   refers to an orbiting object that remains at the same location above the Earth, meaning it orbits at the same speed at which the Earth revolves

g force   g represents the acceleration caused by the force resulting from gravity of a massive body

great circle   an imaginary circle on the surface of a sphere whose plane passes through the center of the sphere

heliocentric   another word for "Sun-centered." The prefix *helio-* is Greek for "Sun."

hyperbolic orbit   descriptive of an orbital object, such as a comet, whose eccentricity is large (greater than 1.0) and therefore will never be gravitationally captured by the object around which it orbits

hypergolic self-igniting, with reference to combinations of chemical fuels and oxidizers and their ability to ignite when brought together

inclination a measurement in degrees of an object's angular plane away from the ecliptic

inferior planets from the perspective of the Earth, these are the planets in our solar system located between the Earth and the Sun that are therefore capable of phases, such as those seen in the Moon, only not as extreme. Venus and Mercury are both inferior planets.

ionosphere the part of the Earth's outer atmosphere where ions and electrons are present in quantities sufficient to affect the propagation of radio waves

Jovian pertaining to the planet Jupiter

kiloparsec a unit of measurement equal to 1,000 parsecs

light-year the distance light travels in one Earth year, equal to 5,880,000,000,000 miles (9.46053×10^{12} km [63,240 AUs])

luminosity the total energy output of a star

lunar module called also the *lunar excursion module* (LEM), this is the part of a spacecraft that carries the astronauts from the command module to the surface of the Moon and back

mach number named after Austrian scientist Ernst Mach (1838–1916), a number expressing the ratio of the speed of a body with respect to the speed of sound

magnification a measure of a lens's ability to increase the size of an image

magnitude a method of measurement developed to describe the brightness of a celestial object

mass ratio the ratio of weight before and after consumption of rocket propellant

meteor a meteoroid that enters the Earth's atmosphere and rapidly burns up. Commonly referred to as a shooting star.

meteorite a meteor that strikes the Earth after failing to completely burn up in the atmosphere

meteoroid a small hunk of space debris prior to any contact with a planetary atmosphere

nadir a point directly opposite the zenith, below the observer

nebulae   a large, diffuse cloud of dust and gas in space

oblate sphere   in astronomy, a spherical object that appears flattened at its poles, typically due to a high rate of rotation. Saturn is an example of an oblate sphere.

occultation   the situation in space when one object, passes in front of another object, resulting in a partial or total obstruction of the view of the farther object

opposition   when the Earth is lined up with one of the superior planets on the same side of the Sun

parallax   the apparent motion of an object against a background due to the motion of the viewer

parsec   the distance of an object that has a celestial parallax of one arc second. One parsec equals 3.26 light-years.

penumbra   pertaining to an eclipse, a partial area of shadow between complete light and complete shadow

periapsis   an object's nearest point to the object it is orbiting

periastron   in a binary system, the position in a star's orbit where it is closest to the other star

perigee   specific to an object's nearest point to the Earth in its orbit

perihelion   specific to an object's nearest point to the Sun in its orbit

phase   the fraction of the illuminated portion of a celestial object visible to a viewer from the object the body is orbiting. A *waxing* Moon is the phase in which illumination grows. A *waning* Moon is the phase in which illumination lessens.

precession of equinoxes   the westward progression of the intersection of the celestial equator and the ecliptic

propellant   fuel and oxidizer used for rocket propulsion

red shift   the reddening of light from a receding star due to the Doppler effect

reflector   a telescope that uses mirrors to focus light from an object

refractor   a telescope that commonly uses glass lenses to focus light from an object

resolution   a measurement of the ability of an astronomical telescope to show fine detail

retrograde pertaining to planetary motion, this is real or apparent westward motion. Retrograde is opposite of direct motion.

right ascension the angular position of a celestial object measured eastward along the celestial equator from vernal equinox to the hour circle of the object

service module the section of a spacecraft containing the main rocket engine, propellant tanks, fuel cells, oxygen, and water

sidereal pertaining or related to stars and their attributes, such as proper motion, luminosity, distances, binary or double, and color

singularity a point in space-time where physical laws are suspended

singularity theorem a theorem that shows a singularity must exist under certain circumstances and, in particular, that the universe must have started with a singularity

space the part of the universe lying outside the limits of the Earth's atmosphere

space-time the combination of four-dimensional space and time

superior planets from the perspective of the Earth, the planets in our solar system located beyond the Earth and the Sun that are therefore incapable of phases

thrust propelling force developed by a rocket engine that is produced by propellant mass flow and exhaust velocity relative to the vehicle

transit in reference to our solar system, it is a celestial object passing in front of another more distant celestial object. In terms of surveying, it pertains to the passage of a celestial body across the observer's meridian

umbra pertaining to an eclipse, the absolute darkest portion of the shadow

wormhole a thin tunnel of space-time thought to connect two distant regions of the universe, possibly providing a means for time travel

zenith the point on the celestial sphere toward which the local vertical is directed, meaning the point directly overhead

zodiac a belt of sky extending about nine degrees to each side of the ecliptic. Since ancient times, the zodiac has been sectioned at intervals of 30 degrees along the ecliptic, each of the sections being designated by a sign of the zodiac. Each sign bears the name of the constellation that it occupied in the second century B.C.E. Precession of the equinoxes has since shifted each constellation forward one sign; thus, while the Sun is said to enter Aries at the vernal equinox, it would actually be entering the constellation Pisces.

FURTHER RESOURCES

Books

Bennett, Jeffery O., Seth Shostak, and Bruce Jakosky. *Life in the Universe*. New York: Pearson Education, 2002. Teaches the nature of science and how to distinguish true science from pseudoscience and examines exobiology, or the possibility of life beyond Earth.

Butrica, Andrew J. *Single Stage to Orbit: Politics, Space Technology, and the Quest for Reusable Rocketry (New Series in NASA History)*. Baltimore: Johns Hopkins University Press, 2003. Discusses the visions of rocket pioneers, their concepts, and the influence of politics on the furthering of this new technology.

Campbell, Ann-Jeanette. *The New York Public Library Amazing Space: A Book of Answers for Kids*. Indianapolis: John Wiley & Sons, 1997. Geared for students in grades 5–8, this is an excellent book on general astronomy that whets the appetite of those eager to understand space science. Includes diagrams.

Crowe, Michael J. *Modern Theories of the Universe: From Herschel to Hubble*. New York: Dover Publications, 1994. An introduction to cosmology from scientific, historical, and philosophical points of view. For high school students and up.

———. *Theories of the World from Antiquity to the Copernican Revolution: Second Revised Edition*. New York: Dover Publications, 2001. Examines the historical evolution of astronomical theory toward heliocentricity from Ptolemy to Galileo. For high school students and up.

Ferguson, Kitty. *Brahe & Kepler: The Unlikely Partnership That Forever Changed Our Understanding of the Heavens*. New York:

Walker and Co., 2002. Lends insight to the dissimilar personalities of Tycho Brahe and Johannes Kepler and their contributions to the furthering of modern science.

Gingrich, Owen. *The Eye of Heaven: Ptolemy, Copernicus, Kepler (Masters of Modern Physics)*. New York: American Institute of Physics, 1993. Compelling writing and brilliant research work by renowned astronomer and science historian Owen Gingrich. Great introduction to the history of astronomy.

Hoskin, Michael. *The Cambridge Concise History of Astronomy.* New York: Cambridge University Press, 1999. Covers the historical highlights of astronomy through modern times. Includes illustrations and photographs.

King, Henry C. *The History of the Telescope.* New York: Dover Publications, 2003. A comprehensive history of the telescope from ancient Egypt to the Hale telescope at Mount Wilson Observatory. Includes photos.

Koestler, Arthur. *The Sleepwalkers: A History of Man's Changing Vision of the Universe.* New York: Arkana, 1989. An excellent biography that outlines the lives of Nicholas Copernicus, Tycho Brahe, Galileo Galilei, and Johannes Kepler.

March, Robert H. *Physics for Poets.* 5th ed. New York: McGraw-Hill, 2002. A brief introduction to the development of modern physics. Expertly written and geared toward those who do not yet have a grasp on the complexities of physics.

Munitz, Milton K. *Theories of the Universe: From Babylonian Myth to Modern Science.* New York: Free Press, 1965. History of the development of humankind's theories about the origins of the universe. Though an older volume, it provides classic information on the Copernican revolution and the cosmological theories of dozens of past astronomers, including Fred Hoyle, Edwin P. Hubble, and Albert Einstien.

Rosen, Edward. *Copernicus and His Successors.* London: Hambledon Press, 1995. An essay on Copernicus, how he was seen by contemporaries, and his relationship to other scientists, including Galileo, Brahe, and Kepler.

Internet Resources

"Arecibo Observatory." Available online. URL: http://www.naic. edu. Accessed November 29, 2004. Located in Arecibo, Puerto Rico, the Arecibo Observatory is part of the National Science Foundation (NSF), whose aim is to promote scientific and engineering progress.

"Ask Us." NASA's Cosmicopia. Available online. URL: http:// helios.gsfc.nasa.gov/physicist.html. Accessed November 29, 2004. Provides complete and comprehensible answers to questions about cosmic and heliospheric science. Includes an extensive list of previously asked questions and an e-mail link to pose new ones.

"Astronomical League." Available online. URL: http://www.astro league.org. Accessed November 29, 2004. An amateur Web-based astronomical organization dedicated to promoting astronomy to the public.

"European Southern Observatory." Available online. URL: http:// www.eso.org. Accessed November 29, 2004. Headquartered near Munich in Garching, Germany, the European Southern Observatory is an intergovernmental European organization for astronomical research that includes 10 member countries.

"The Faces of Science: African Americans in the Sciences." Princeton University. Available online. URL: http://www.princeton.edu/ ~mcbrown/display/faces.html. Accessed November 29, 2004. Profiles African-American men and women who have contributed to the advancement of science and engineering.

"Famous Astronomers and Astrophysicists." Kent State University. Available online. URL: http://cnr2.kent.edu/~manley/astron omers.html. Accessed November 29, 2004. An alphabetical index of scientists with links that direct the reader to other informative sites.

"History of Women." United States Naval Observatory. Available online. URL: http://maia.usno.navy.mil/women_history/history. html. Accessed November 29, 2004. Contributions made by women to the U.S. Naval Observatory.

"Lowell Observatory." Available online. URL: http://www.lowell. edu. Accessed November 29, 2004. Located in Flagstaff, Arizona,

Lowell Observatory is a privately owned astronomical research institution founded in 1894 by American mathematician Percival Lowell, best known for his discovery of the planet Pluto.

"MacTutor History of Mathematics Archive." University of Saint Andrews. Available online. URL: http://www-groups.dcs.st-and.ac.uk/~history. Accessed November 29, 2004. A searchable online index of mathematical history and the biographies of famous mathematicians, from the University of Saint Andrews, Scotland.

"Mount Wilson Observatory." Available online. URL: http://www.mtwilson.edu. Accessed November 29, 2004. Founded in December 1904 by George Ellery Hale, the Mount Wilson Observatory, located in the San Gabriel Mountains of California, is an astronomical research organization and is known as the most powerful existing facility for the observation of the Sun.

"National Aeronautics and Space Administration (NASA) Earth Observatory." Available online. URL: http://www.earthobservatory.nasa.gov. Accessed November 29, 2004. NASA's mission is to provide a freely accessible publication on the Internet where the public can obtain new satellite imagery and scientific information about the Earth.

"National Aeronautics and Space Administration (NASA) History Office." Available online. URL: http://www.hq.nasa.gov/office/pao/History. Accessed November 29, 2004. The History Office was established in 1959, a year after NASA itself was formed, to document and preserve the agency's history.

"Solar and Heliospheric Observatory (SOHO)." Available online. URL: http://soho.nascom.nasa.gov. Accessed November 29, 2004. A cooperative effort between the European Space Agency (ESA) and National Aeronautics and Space Administration (NASA), the observatory's goal is the detailed study of the Sun.

"Tycho Brahe Observatory." Available online. URL: http://www.tbobs.lu.se. Accessed November 29, 2004. The Tycho Brahe observatory is an amateur facility located outside Malmö, in southern Sweden. It is run by the Astronomical Society Tycho Brahe (ASTB).

"United States Naval Observatory." Available online. URL: http://www.usno.navy.mil. Accessed November 29, 2004. The U.S. Naval Observatory is the preeminent authority in the areas of precise time and astrometry, and distributes Earth orientation parameters and other astronomical data required for accurate navigation and fundamental astronomy.

"Women Astronomers." The Woman Astronomer Homepage. Available online. URL: http://www.womanastronomer.com/women_astronomers.htm. Accessed November 29, 2004. An online index of women scientists covering three categories: historical, current professional, and amateur women astronomers.

Periodicals

Astronomy
21027 Crossroads Circle
P.O. Box 1612
Waukesha, WI 53187
Telephone: (800) 558-1544
www.astronomy.com
A popular astronomy magazine that assists readers in exploring the universe from home by offering tips on telescope observing and astrophotography.

Discover
114 Fifth Avenue
New York, NY 10011
Telephone: (212) 633-4400
www.discover.com
A popular monthly magazine containing easy-to-understand articles on a variety of scientific topics.

Odyssey
Cobblestone Publishing Company
30 Grove Street, Suite C
Peterborough, NH 03458

Telephone: (800) 821-0115
www.odysseymagazine.com
An award-winning science magazine for young readers that features articles on astronomy and space exploration as well as other branches of science.

Scientific American
415 Madison Avenue
New York, NY 10017
Telephone: (212) 754-0550
www.sciam.com
A popular monthly magazine that publishes articles on a broad range of subjects and current issues in science and technology.

Sky and Telescope Magazine
49 Bay State Road
Cambridge, MA 02138-1200
Telephone: (800) 253-0245
www.skyandtelescope.com
Monthly publication featuring the latest developments in astronomy, including news and events.

Societies and Organizations

Aerospace Education Foundation (http://www.aef.org) 1501 Lee Highway, Arlington, VA, 22209-1198. Telephone: (703) 247-5839. A nonprofit organization whose goals are to further aerospace advances in the United States through public awareness programs, education, and financial assistance.

Ames Research Center (http://www.arc.nasa.gov) Moffett Field, CA, 94035. Telephone: (650) 604-4191. Originally founded in 1939, Ames Research Center, a division of NASA, specializes in research into new knowledge and technologies that support NASA interests.

The Benjamin Banneker Association, Michigan State University (http://www.math.msu.edu/banneker/goal.html) P.O. Box 24182,

Lansing, MI, 48909-4182. The goal of the Benjamin Banneker Association is to promote the educational and professional needs of its members and to further the educational and developmental needs of African-American children in mathematics.

Canadian Aeronautics and Space Institute (http://www.casi.ca) 1750 Courtwood Crescent, Suite 105, Ottawa, Ontario, Canada, K2C 2B5. Telephone: (613) 234-0191. Formed in 1962 to advance the art, science, engineering, and applications of aeronautics and space in Canada.

Goddard Institute for Space Studies (GISS), Columbia University (http://www.giss.nasa.gov) 2880 Broadway, New York, NY, 10025. Telephone: (212) 678-5500. A division of NASA, GISS emphasizes a broad study of global change, including climate modeling, Earth observations, climate impacts, and planetary atmospheres.

Institute and Museum of the History of Science (http://galileo.imss. firenze.it) Piazza dei Giudici, 1, 50122 Florence, Italy. Telephone: +39 055 265311. Leading international institution combining a noted museum that includes scientific instruments of Galileo's, such as his astrolabe, compass, and telescope. The institute is dedicated to the research, documentation, and circulation of the history of science.

Jet Propulsion Laboratory (JPL) (http://www.jpl.nasa.gov) 4800 Oak Grove Drive, Pasadena, CA, 91109. Telephone: (818) 354-9314. Jet Propulsion Laboratory is managed by the California Institute of Technology and manages the robotic exploration of the solar system for NASA.

Marshall Space Flight Center (http://www.msfc.nasa.gov) CD 70, Huntsville, AL, 35812. Telephone: (256)-544-0034. Established in 1960 to develop the *Saturn* rockets. Wernher von Braun was its first director. Today, its mission is to further the implementation of technology that will promote scientific discoveries in space. Marshall Space Flight Center is a branch of NASA.

The Mars Society (http://www.marssociety.org) P.O. Box 273, Indian Hills, CO 80454. The purpose of the Mars Society is to further the exploration and settlement of Mars through public outreach and by providing support for both private and government projects.

National Academy of Sciences (http://www.nationalacademies. org) 500 Fifth Street NW, Washington, DC, 20001. Telephone: (202) 334-1602. The National Academy of Sciences is a private, nonprofit society engaged in scientific and engineering research and dedicated to the furtherance of science and technology.

National Aeronautics and Space Administration (NASA) (http://www.nasa.gov) NASA Headquarters, 300 E Street SW, Washington, DC, 20024-3210. Telephone: (202) 358-0000. Founded in 1958, NASA's first assignment was the Mercury program, to test the feasibility of putting a human in space, and the organization has been expanding ever since. NASA Headquarters manages the space flight centers, research centers, and other installations that constitute NASA.

National Space Society (http://www.nss.org) 1620 I Street NW, Suite 615, Washington, DC, 20006. Telephone: (202) 429-1600. Founded in 1974 by Wernher von Braun, the NSS has as its vision people living, working, and thriving in communities beyond the Earth.

Nicolas Copernicus Astronomical Center (http://www.camk.edu. pl/eng) Bartycka 18, 00-716 Warsaw, Poland. Telephone: +48 22 8410041. The Nicolas Copernicus Astronomical Center is an institute of the Polish Academy of Sciences, founded in 1978. Fields of research cover astronomy, astrophysics, and cosmology.

The Planetary Society (http://www.planetary.org) 65 North Catalina Avenue, Pasadena, CA, 91106-2301. Telephone: (626) 793-5100. The Planetary Society is a nonprofit, nongovernmental organization founded in 1980 by Carl Sagan, Bruce Murray, and Louis Friedman to encourage the exploration of the solar system and the search for extraterrestrial life.

The Royal Astronomical Society (http://www.ras.org.uk) Burlington House, Piccadilly, London W1J 0BQ, UK. Telephone: +44 020 7734 4582. The Royal Astronomical Society is Britain's foremost professional organization for astronomy and astrophysics, geophysics, solar and solar-terrestrial physics, and planetary sciences.

The Royal Society of London (http://www.royalsoc.ac.uk) 6–9 Carlton House Terrace, London, SW1Y 5AG, UK. Telephone:

+44 020 7451 2500. Founded in 1660, the Royal Society of London represents and honors contributions within the scientific community in Britain and across the world.

Space Camp (http://www.spacecamp.com) U.S. Space and Rocket Center, Tranquility Base, P.O. Box 070015 Huntsville, AL, 35807-7015. Telephone: (256) 837-3400. U.S. Space Camp began operations in 1982 as a five-day program dedicated to training young people who are interested in space. Activities include simulated space shuttle missions, movies, training simulators, rocket building and launches, scientific experiments, and lectures on the past, present, and future of space exploration.

United Kingdom Rocketry Association (UKRA) (http://www.ukra.org.uk) P.O. Box 1561, Sheffield S11 7XA, UK. Established in 1996 to promote model and high-power rocketry at all levels and provide encouragement and inspiration to future generations of rocketeers.

The William Herschel Museum (http://www.bath-preservation-trust.org.uk/museums/herschel) 19 New King Street, Bath BA1 2BL, UK. The Web site contains a virtual tour of the museum, plus biographies, events, information, and a search engine.

Index

189